French

Key Words

and Expressions

The Combined Book

Saul H. Rosenthal

French Key Words and Expressions: The Combined Book

Published by Wheatmark®
610 East Delano Street, Suite 104, Tucson, Arizona 85705 U.S.A.
www.wheatmark.com

ISBN: 978-1-60494-247-7
LCCN: 2009920897

Also by Saul H. Rosenthal

The Rules for **the Gender of French Nouns**, (3rd revised edition)

Speaking Better French, **Faux Amis**

Speaking Better French, **more Faux Amis**

Speaking Better French, **still more Faux Amis**

French Faux Amis: The Combined Book

Speaking Better French, **The Key Words and Expressions**

Speaking Better French, **More Key Words and Expressions**

et en français

Les règles du genre des noms *au masculin et au féminin*

Mieux parler anglais, **Faux amis**

Acknowledgements

So many people helped me in writing this book, and the two books of key words and expressions which are combined in it, that it's difficult to try to thank them without forgetting some of them. Some people suggested expressions and words, some answered my questions about their correct usage in French, and some people kindly read over partial or entire manuscripts to look for errors or misstatements.

I wish to thank Catherine Ostrow and Sylvie Shurgot, Jean-Claude and Marie-Jo Parfait, Brigitte Humbert, Jean-Marc Bard, John Moran, and Marie-Claire and Jean Lubaszka, who all helped me with some aspect of the preparation of these books.

As always, my daughter Sadie was available when I had questions about how cetain words and expressions are used.

I also appreciated the encouraging words I received from Norman Shapiro, John Romeiser, Jonathan Walsh, Christiane Laeufer, Judy Baughin, A. G. Fralin, Marion Vergues, Roger Hawkins, and Steve Hedge as well as many others, including the anonymous people who gave my books great reviews on amazon.com and elsewhere.

My wife Cindy suggested many key words and expressions and was wonderfully patient while I worked away on writing these books. She's the best. I'm a lucky guy.

To all of you, and anyone else that I missed, thanks again very much.

Contents

Introduction

These key words and expressions were originally included in two separate books entitled:

Speaking Better French, The Key Words and Expressions You'll Need Every Day

Speaking Better French, More Key Words and Expressions

Since there were many essential and necessary words in each of the two books, I felt that it would be much more convenient for you if I were to combine them into one book. This is the book!

In addition I've updated, edited, and rewritten the key words, and I've added additional words that weren't in either of the first two books.

Well, you may ask, why a book of key words at all?

Let me start my response by quoting from a reviewer, on amazon.com, of the first of the above books:

Perhaps the most amazing thing about this book is that

it took until 2007 for anyone to think of writing it! The author's insight is right on target. This book does indeed fill a huge and inexplicable gap in the otherwise very crowded market for books on learning French. (Come to think of it, I haven't found such books in any of the three foreign languages I've studied besides French.)

Now I'll continue by you what this book isn't. It isn't a book about learning vocabulary, about learning nouns and verbs.

Then what is it? It's a book to help you talk more fluent, colloquial French, the French that French people use.

It gives you the key words and little expressions that are used all the time in day-to-day conversation. These are the words that make the language flow. I discuss each one separately and tell you how to use it.

For each key word or expression I also usually give you a number of examples using it in sentences so you can see how it's normally used. That way, it won't be just a meaningless term for you to memorize.

There are thousands of idioms in French, but many of them are used just occasionally and for very specific occasions.

Take, for instance, the English expressions "There are many ways to skin a cat" and "He's sowing his wild oats". They are nice to know, and there are specific circumstances where they are appropriate to use. However, you could get along very well most of your life in English without knowing those idioms.

French has lots of idioms like that too. *Il fait les quatre cent coups* is pretty close to "He's sowing his wild oats". It's nice

2

if you know it, but you can get along very well without it. It's an idiom that you might encounter just once or twice in your lifetime. If you studied it, you might be able to recognize it if you heard it, but you probably would never recall it fast enough to use it yourself.

However there are other key words and expressions in French that are used all the time. They are the French equivalents of English expressions like *in spite of, just in case, as soon as, on the other hand, by the way, all the same, Who knows!, No way!, So what?,* and many, many more.

As opposed to idioms like "sowing his wild oats", which are restricted to once or twice in a lifetime situations, these expressions are multipurpose. They serve in an infinite number of daily situations. You not only need to recognize them, **you need to use them yourself** in daily speech.

These key words are the subjects of this book. Some of them are actual short idioms. Most are simply the words that grease the wheels of French conversation.

While the first goal of the book is to give you these little words and expressions that make the language flow, the second goal of the book is to help you talk and understand spoken French.

When I say spoken French, I mean the way people really talk. Some expressions that French people use are very informal, they use shortcuts, and they are not what you would call standard or proper French. It's similar to the same informal devices we use in English.

When we say "See you tomorrow!" there is no subject in that

sentence. The "I will" has been dropped. We know it's not proper English and we wouldn't use it in a formal letter or a formal interview, but that's the way we often talk.

Most French people use the same kind of abbreviations in casual speech. Most of my French friends think of it as "spoken French", as opposed to "written French", and they accept it as normal, depending on the circumstances.

The French in general tend to be much more purist about their language than we are about English. They've had grammar pounded into their heads when they were in school and they know immediately which form is standard French. However, when they are speaking they use spoken French, which is different. This book will help you to understand and speak spoken French the way the French speak it.

Consider the expression *"C'est pas vrai !"* It's not standard French because the *"ne"* is dropped, as often happens in spoken French. In standard written French it should be: *"Ce n'est pas vrai"*. However, in practice almost no one says *Ce n'est pas vrai !* The usual spoken expression is: *C'est pas vrai !* When an expression like *"C'est pas vrai"* is in common use, and when this is the overwhelming way that it's used orally, I include it that way in the book.

You must be aware, however, that in formal situations, and when you are writing something formal, you must use standard French. To help you remember, where I use informal spoken French like this in the book, I usually call it to your attention in the text with a little reminder that this is spoken French, and that it should not be used in more formal situations.

4

I hope that you will find this book remarkable and *éclatant*. My goal has been not only to make it a great resource, but also to make it enjoyable to read. I hope that it'll be fun for you. You might think that fun is an odd word to use for a book that you will use for learning, but this book will be fun!

Key Words and Expressions

I have not alphabetized these key words on purpose. This is not meant to be dictionary. My hope is that these expressions will interest and surprise you as you encounter them, and that the book will be a voyage of discovery and a pleasure to read. And, rest assured, there is an alphabetical listing of the expressions in the back of the book for reference, in case you have need of it.

Please note that when there is dialogue, in most cases I have adopted the convention of placing a dash between the two speakers. For example:

Tu peux venir ? --- J'espère bien !

Let's begin:

Qui sait !

Qui sait ! means <u>Who knows</u>!. You can use it in the same way that you'd use "Who knows!" in English.

À combien vont ils arriver ? --- Qui sait !

How many will show up? --- Who knows!

Où se trouve votre fils aujourd'hui ? --- Qui sait !

Where's your son today? --- Who knows!

Va savoir !

Like *Qui sait*, **Va savoir** theoretically could be translated as <u>Who knows</u>! However while *Qui sait !* can be used for any unknown simple fact, *Va savoir !* has more the feeling of an unsolved (and unsolvable) small mystery. It means something more like <u>We'll never know</u>!

Est-ce qu'elle a vraiment fait ça ? --- Va savoir !

Did she really do that? --- We'll never know.

Pourquoi est-ce qu'il a dit ça ? --- Va savoir !

Why did he say that? --- We'll never know. That's just the kind of person he is.

Va savoir ce qu'il a contre moi.

I have no idea what he has against me.

quant à ...

The expression **quant à** means <u>as for</u> or <u>with regard to</u>. *Quant à* often, but not always, begins a sentence. As with most of these expressions, *quant à* is versatile in that it can be used in many different circumstances:

> **Quant à moi, je suis d'accord.**
>
> As for me, I agree.

> **Quant à cette maison, c'est trop chère.**
>
> As for that house, it's too expensive.

> **Quant à la morale, elle ne me préoccupe guère. Je vous scandalise ?**
>
> As for morals, I don't worry about them much. Do I shock you? (from *Les Thibault* by Roger Martin du Gard)

> **Quant à y aller le nuit, personne n'ose le faire.**
>
> As for going there at night, nobody dares to do it.

par hasard

Par hasard means <u>by accident</u> or <u>by chance</u>.

> **Je l'ai rencontré par hasard.**
>
> I met him by chance.

Est-ce que, par hasard, tu pourrais le faire pour moi ?

Can you do it for me, by any chance?

Par le plus grand des hasards j'ai retrouvé ce livre.

By extraordinary luck I found this book again.

By an extraordinary accident I found this book again.

pourvu que

Pourvu que means <u>Provided that</u> or <u>Let's hope that</u> and it expresses a wish. It usually starts a sentence or clause and is used with the subjunctive of the next verb.

Pourvu qu'elle arrive à l'heure ! Nous pourrions alors manger avant huit heures.

Let's hope that she arrives on time. If so we can eat before eight o'clock.

Provided that she arrives on time we'll be able to eat before eight o'clock.

Pourvu qu'il puisse venir !

Let's hope that he can come!

Pourvu qu'il fasse beau !

Let's hope that the weather is good!

Side Note: You'll notice that *Pourvu que* is a figurative use of the verb *pourvoir* which means to provide (*Pourvu que* / Provided that).

Quel... !

Quel...! is an exclamation, translated as <u>What a</u>...! and usually expressing admiration as in:

Quel repas délicieux!

What a delicious meal!

Quelle femme !

What a woman!

This expression can, however, sometimes express a negative sentiment as in:

Quel désastre !

What a disaster!

Quelle horreur !!!

Quelle Horreur ! is a very French expression and is usually spoken with lots of emotion and emphasis. It means, naturally: <u>That's horrible!</u> or <u>How horrible!</u>

Elle a vraiment dit ça ? Quelle horreur !!!

She really said that? How horrible!

un sacré...

When the adjective **sacré** is placed after the noun it modifies it means <u>sacred</u>. For example: *un édifice sacré.*

However, in casual spoken French, when you place *sacré* before the noun as an exclamation and call something *un sacré...* it means <u>a heck of a...</u>, or more vulgarly, <u>a damn...</u>

This may sound a little confusing, but it will be clearer with a few examples:

> **C'était un sacré travail.**

> It was a heck of a (tough) job.

> **Pierre est un sacré casse-pieds !**

> Pierre is a damn pain in the neck.

> **Sacré Maurice, il nous étonnera toujours !**

> Maurice is incredible, he always astonishes us!

> Good old Maurice, he keeps astonishing us!

trop

Trop usually means <u>too much</u> and thus has a slightly negative connotation.

However, when *trop* is used to modify a positive adjective or adverb, and when spoken with enthusiasm, it doesn't mean "too much". On the contrary, *trop* intensifies the positive adjective or adverb and can be translated more like <u>wonderfully</u> or <u>extraordinarily</u>.

This is a very slangy usage, but it's used all the time in everyday speech, especially by young people.

>*Ta robe est trop belle !*

>*Il est trop beau !*

>*Ce film était trop bien !*

>*Le poisson est trop bon !*

>*Elle est trop mignonne !*

>*Il est trop sympa !*

>*Trop beau !*

>*Trop bon !*

Je veux bien

Je veux bien means <u>I'd be glad to</u> but is often used with a <u>but</u> when there is some obstacle to you doing it, as in:

>*Je veux bien le faire mais je n'ai pas le temps.*

>>I'd be glad to do it but I don't have the time.

Je veux bien les arroser mais je ne trouve pas le tuyau.

I'd be glad to water them but I can't find the hose.

Je veux bien conduire mais je ne connais pas la route.

I'd be glad to drive but I don't know the route.

Je veux bien can also be used as a completely positive response, again meaning I'd be glad to.

Est-ce que tu peux le faire pour moi ? --- Oui, je veux bien !

Could you do it for me? --- Yes, I'd be glad to!

Veux-tu venir ? --- Oui, je veux bien !

Do you want to come? --- Yes, I'd love to!

D'accord !

D'accord is the French equivalent of okay or I agree. It's used all the time and you will find occasions to use it many times a day.

D'accord is short for *Je suis d'accord*. You can usually use either one. *Je suis d'accord* is just a little more formal. For example:

*Je suis d'accord pour le Restaurant Pro-
vençal.*

I agree for the Restaurant Provençal.

*On va au Restaurant Provençal ce soir ?
--- D'accord.*

Shall we go to the Restaurant Provençal
this evening? --- Okay.

*Est-ce que tu peux acheter du pain pour
moi ? --- D'accord.*

Can you buy some bread for me? ---
Okay.

Je ne suis pas d'accord.

I don't agree.

Ils sont d'accord.

They agree. They are in agreement.

In <u>very</u> slangy speech you may even hear *d'accord*
added to the americanism "okay", as in:

Okay, d'accord !

or even, believe it or not:

Okay, d'ac !

I would recommend that you **don't** use *okay d'accord*,
even if you should hear it from others. You are, after
all, trying to sound more French, not American.

C'est pas évident

C'est pas évident means <u>It's not evident or obvious</u> <u>how to do it (or even whether it can be done at all)</u>. This can be boiled down to <u>It won't be easy.</u>

Or it can have a slightly different shade of meaning: <u>It's doubtful. It might not work</u>.

> *On peut peut-être le faire, mais c'est pas évident.*
>
> > Maybe it can be done, but it's not obvious / but I doubt it / but I'm not sure / but it won't be easy.
>
> *Se débrouiller avec l'informatique, c'est pas évident.*
>
> > Figuring everything out about computers isn't easy / isn't obvious.
>
> *Est-ce que tu crois qu'on peut nager ici ? --- Avec autant de rochers, c'est pas évident.*
>
> > Do you think that one can swim here? --- With so many rocks I'm not sure.

Although the *ne* is usually dropped from *C'est pas évident* in **spoken** French, it would not be considered standard French. If you're in a more formal situation you must say: *Ce n'est pas évident.*

16

c'est-à-dire

You use the expression *c'est-à-dire* to make something that you have already said more precise. You could translate it by <u>that is</u>, or by <u>that is to say</u>, (which turns out to be the literal translation).

> *J'arriverai à l'heure prévue. C'est-à-dire, à huit heure pile.*
>
>> I'll arrive at the agreed upon time. That is to say right at eight o'clock.
>
> *Pour me baigner dans la piscine, je préfère que l'eau soit plutôt chaude. C'est-à-dire, plus de vingt-six degrés.*
>
>> To swim in the pool I prefer the water to be rather warm. That is to say, more than twenty-six degrees.
>
> *Le lendemain, c'est-à-dire mardi, nous sommes allés...*
>
>> The next day, that is, Tuesday, we went...

C'est-à-dire ? (with a question mark) means <u>Could you clarify?</u> or <u>Could you be more precise?</u>. For example:

> *La réponse est arrivé trois semaines après l'envoi de ma lettre.*
>
> *C'est-à-dire ?*

Début décembre.

Note that in more formal language one would say *Au début de décembre*, but in spoken French you'd be more likely to hear *Début décembre*.

à savoir

À savoir means <u>namely</u>, or <u>that is to say</u>, and thus is a synonym for *c'est-à-dire*.

> **Il lui manque quelque chose d'essentiel, à savoir l'intelligence.**
>
>> He lacks something essential, namely intelligence.
>>
>> He lacks something essential, that's to say: intelligence.
>>
>> He lacks something essential, if you want to know: intelligence.
>
> **Ils ont beaucoup d'avantages. --- À savoir ?**
>
>> They have alot of advantages. --- That's to say? / Namely? / Could you clarify?

j'ai ouï dire (que)

While some of our expressions come from casual French, using *j'ai ouï dire* may give people the impression that you speak an unusually refined and elegant French. It comes from an old classic French verb, *ouïr* (to hear), which is now mostly obsolete except for this expression. The sense of hearing, however, is still called *l'ouïe*.

J'ai ouï dire means <u>I've heard it said</u>, and usually refers to a rumor or to a word-of-mouth piece of information.

> **J'ai ouï dire que sa soeur est très belle.**
>
>> I've heard it said that his sister is very beautiful.

> **J'ai ouï dire que il est très malin.**
>
>> I've heard that he's very shrewd.

> **J'ai ouï dire que tu veux vendre ta maison.**
>
>> I've heard that you want to sell your house.

A French synonym for *j'ai ouï dire* would be *j'ai entendu dire*.

Il s'agit (de)

The verb *agir* by itself means to act or to take an action, but **il s'agit (de)** is translated <u>it's a question of,</u> or <u>it's about,</u> or <u>it's a matter of</u>. It's a very common expression and you will hear it all the time.

> **De quoi s'agit-il ? or Il s'agit de quoi ?**
>
>> What's it about? What's it a question of? What's the matter?

Il s'agit de ma santé.

It deals with my health / It's about my health.

Il s'agit de Jacques.

It's about Jacques.

Il ne s'agit pas d'argent.

It's not a question of money / It's not about money.

Quand il s'agit de boire un coup, il est toujours le premier.

When it's a question of having a drink, he's always the first.

à peu près

The French expression **à peu près** means <u>just about, approximately, more-or-less, nearly, pretty close to.</u> It's used in expressions like:

Il est à peu près certain que...

It's almost certain that...

Le restaurant était à peu près vide.

The restaurant was practically empty.

Il y avait à peu près cinquante personnes dans le magasin.

There were close to fifty people in the store.

faire les courses
faire du shopping

Faire les courses means to <u>run errands</u> or go shopping for food and supplies. You will use it, or hear it, just about every day.

> *Nous allons faire les courses demain matin.*

> We are going to run our errands tomorrow morning.

If you are talking about <u>wandering about shopping malls</u> and shopping for clothes, that's *faire du shopping*.

> *Ma femme aime beaucoup faire du shopping, moi pas du tout.*

> My wife likes very much to go shopping but I don't like it at all.

Faire du shopping is of course imported from English and a French language purist might be aghast to find it in a book, but I'm giving you what people really say. And, they do say *faire du shopping*.

C'est pas vrai !

The expression *C'est pas vrai !* is said with incredulity and astonishment, and with an accent on the "*C'est*" and one especially on the "*vrai*". Either the "*C'est*" or the "*vrai !*", or both, may be slightly drawn out, depending on the dramatic flair of the speaker.

C'est pas vrai ! means something like It can't be true! or You've got to be kidding! It's wonderfully expressive.

> **Elle a vraiment dit ça ? C'est pas vrai !**

>> She really said that? You've got to be kidding!

Jamais de la vie !

Translating **Jamais de la vie** word for word it means "Never in my life". Colloquially, you'd translate it as something like No way! or Not a chance!

> **Ta mère veut venir vivre chez nous? Jamais de la vie !**

>> Your mother wants to come live with us? No way!

Impeccable !

Impeccable can mean perfectly dressed or perfectly clean, as in English.

> **un complet impeccable**

>> a suit of clothes perfect for the occasion (and attractive, clean and uncrushed)

However, in casual French **impeccable !** is often used, either in a sentence or as a freestanding exclamation, to mean <u>perfect</u> or <u>great</u>.

> **Comment était le diner ? --- Impeccable !**

> How was the dinner? --- Perfect! / Great!

> **C'est impeccable, ton idée / Ton idée est impeccable.**

> Your idea is sensational / great.

In very casual speech, especially among young people, *Impeccable !* is sometimes shortened to *Impec !*

> **Je peux arriver à vingt heures. --- Impec !**

> I can arrive at eight o'clock. --- Perfect! / That's great!

Side Note: Whereas in English impeccable is pronounced with an accent on the "pecc" and the "able" is somewhat swallowed, in French, the *"ab"* at least of the *"able"*, is fully pronounced.

tant pis

The expression **tant pis** can mean <u>Too bad!</u> or <u>So much the worse!</u>, (which is it's literal translation). It is often used in a light vein, slightly humorously.

> **Nous ne pouvons pas aller avec vous au**

> *restaurant ce soir. --- Tant pis pour vous, c'est un très bon resto.*

> We can't go with you to the restaurant this evening. --- Too bad for you. It's a very good restaurant.

> *Il ne veut pas se balader avec nous. --- Tant pis pour lui !*

> He doesn't want to go walking with us. --- Too bad for him. (It's him that's missing out.)

Sometimes *tant pis* can just mean <u>too bad, never mind, don't worry, it's not a big deal</u>. (You can tell from context and tone of voice.)

> *Désolé, je peux pas jouer au tennis avec vous demain. --- Oh, dommage ! Tant pis.*

> Sorry, I can't play tennis with you tomorrow. --- Oh! Too bad, never mind, don't worry.

Note that the *ne* was left out of the *je peux pas* in the last example. I know that I've explained it before but this is casual French. In more formal situations you'd have to say: <u>Je suis désolé, mais je ne peux pas jouer...</u>

tant mieux

> **Tant mieux** is the opposite of *tant pis*. *Tant mieux* means <u>So much the better!</u>

Jean peut venir avec nous demain. --- Tant mieux, j'aime marcher avec lui.

Jean can come with us tomorrow. --- So much the better. I like walking with him.

voire

The adverb **voire** is used when you have made an assertion and you want to make it stronger. *Voire* can be translated as <u>even</u> or <u>indeed</u>. It's a very useful expression. Here are some examples which will clarify what I mean:

Elle est agaçante, voire horrible, de temps en temps.

She's annoying, even horrible, from time to time.

Durant des mois, voire des années...

For months, even years...

Dire cela est inutile, voire dangereux.

To say that is useless, indeed dangerous / To say that is useless, even dangerous.

Voire has nothing to do with the verb *voir* (to see).

Elle est comment ? or Comment est-elle ?

Elle est comment ? can mean <u>What's she like</u>?,

What kind of person is she?, or What does she look like?. It's used only for people, not for places or things.

Elle est comment, ta copine ?

> What is your girlfriend like? And what does she look like?

Ton frère, comment est-il ?

> What's your brother like? What kind of person is he? (or "How's your brother's health?" if the speaker knew that your brother had been ill).

bien (used to intensify)

The adverb **bien** is often used to intensify another adverb or an adjective. It can be translated as quite, very, or really. A French synonym would be *vraiment*.

Here are some examples of the use of *bien* to modify an adverb or an adjective:

Elle est bien jeune.

> She's quite young / She's very young.

C'est bien assez.

> It's quite enough / It's really enough.

C'est bien mieux.

It's <u>really</u> better / It's <u>much</u> better.

Here are some examples of the use of *bien* to modify various verbs.

> ### *Tu peux venir ? --- J'espère bien !*
>
> Can you come? --- I really hope so.
>
> ### *J'espère bien y aller.*
>
> I really hope to go.
>
> ### *Je veux bien le faire.*
>
> I'm quite willing to do it. I really want to do it.
>
> ### *Il faut bien le faire.*
>
> It's really necessary to do it.
>
> ### *Il me semble bien que...*
>
> It really seems to me that...
>
> ### *Paul est bien venu, n'est-ce pas ?*
>
> Paul really came, didn't he? Paul did come, didn't he?

Note that in other contexts, bien means <u>well</u>.

> ### *Nous allons bien manger.*
>
> We will eat well.
>
> ### *J'ai bien dormi.*

I have slept well.

correct

You can use the French adjective **correct** to mean accurate or correct as in English.

> **Toutes ses réponses ont été correctes.**

> All her answers were correct.

However, *correct* can also often mean proper, polite or honest in dealings.

> **Il a été correct avec Jean.**

> He was polite and fair with Jean.

> **M. Blanc est toujours correct en affaires.**

> Mr. Blanc is always honest in business dealings.

However, in spoken French, *correct* has another meaning. If you are talking, for example, about a restaurant, a hotel, a meal or a wine, *c'était correct* means that it was acceptable and reasonable, and that there was nothing wrong with it, but that it was not special. For example:

> **Comment était le restaurant hier soir? --- euh... C'était correct.**

> This lets you know that the restaurant was passable and okay, but not special.

exceptionnellement

in English, exceptionally means "unusually" (as in exceptionally hot) or "exceedingly" (as in exceptionally intelligent). ***Exceptionnellement*** can have these same meanings in French.

However, the way you are most likely to encounter *exceptionnellement* is different than what you would expect from English. In French, *exceptionnellement* often means <u>for this time only</u>, or <u>by way of an exception</u>. For example:

> ***Le magasin est exceptionnellement fermé ce mardi pour raisons familiales.***

> > The store is closed this Tuesday only, for family reasons.

donc

Donc is an expressive word much used in spoken French. Although its meaning is almost always evident when I hear it, it's difficult to define exactly. I'll do my best, and then give you some examples which I hope will clarify the usage.

The first meaning of *donc* is <u>thus</u> or <u>therefore</u>. After an initial thought, *donc* introduces the conclusion which is a consequence of the initial thought.

> ***Je pense, donc je suis.***

> > I think, therefore I am. (Déscartes)

Il a téléphoné pour dire qu'il est très en retard, donc nous allons manger sans lui.

He telephoned to say that he will be very delayed, therefore we will eat without him.

Il a trois grandes maisons, il est donc assez riche.

He has three big houses. He is thus fairly rich.

The second usage of donc is <u>to give emphasis</u> or to reinforce a question or an exclamation. It may express surprise in this usage. It can be translated as <u>thus</u>, but it can often be almost omitted in the translation.

C'est donc ici que tu travailles ?

It's (thus) here that you work? So this is where you work? (with surprise)

Qu'est-ce que vous voulez, donc ?

What (exactly) do you want? (Said with empahsis in an upset tone of voice.)

Donc, il n'est pas venu ?

(Thus), he didn't come !? (with incredulity).

Taisez-vous, donc!

Shut up, will you !?

Dans sa déposition, donc, elle prétend qu'elle n'était pas là.

In her deposition, thus, she claims that she wan't there.

C'est cela que je ne comprends pas. --- Mais quoi donc ?

It's that that I don't understand. --- But *what,* exactly?

Finally, it is used <u>after an interruption to come back to the subject</u>.

Vous disiez donc que...

Thus, you were saying that...

par contre
en revanche
au contraire

Par contre means <u>on the other hand</u>, and you can use it just as you would use "on the other hand" in English.

Il n'est pas très intelligent. Par contre, il est rusé.

He's not very intelligent. On the other hand, he's cunning / shrewd.

En revanche is a near synonym for *par contre,* and also means <u>on the other hand</u>.

La mobylette a un pneu crevé, mais en re-vanche le vélo est en état de marche. Si tu veux tu peux le prendre.

The moped has a flat tire but on the other hand the bicycle is ready to go. If you like, you can take it.

The expression **au contraire** is slightly different, as it means <u>on the contrary</u> and expresses more opposition.

Jacques n'est pas intelligent. --- Au con-traire! Je le trouve très intelligent.

Jacques isn't intelligent. --- On the contrary, I find him very intelligent.

en contrepartie

The expression **en contrepartie** can also be translated as <u>on the other hand</u>.

However, *en contrepartie* doesn't have quite the same meaning as *par contre* or *en revanche*, even though they can be translated the same way in English. *En contrepartie* means <u>in compensation for</u> or <u>in return</u>, implying that while something was taken away, something else was figuratively added to balance it or compensate for it: For example:

Le vent avait commencé à souffler fort. En contrepartie la pluie avait cessé.

The wind had started to blow strongly.

On the other hand the rain had stopped /
In compensation, the rain had stopped.

Elle n'était pas jolie, mais en contrepartie elle était intelligente et sympathique.

She wasn't pretty, but in compensation, she was intelligent and likeable.

En contrepartie is a bit more sophisticated expression than *par contre* and you'll hear it less often in common speech.

Mettons que...
Disons que...

These two expressions mean <u>Let's say that</u>, and they are used just as you would use "Let's say that" in English: in other words, to express the thought "Let's start with this supposition or hypothesis and let's see what comes next."

Mettons que je vienne le semaine prochaine. Qu'est-ce que nous allons faire ?

Let's say that can I could come next week. What is it that we are going to do?

Disons qu'il l'a fait. Il faut savoir pourquoi.

Let's say that he did it. We need to know why.

Note that *mettons que* uses the subjunctive of the next verb, *(je vienne* in the example above).

As an aside, *mettons que* comes from the verb *admettre*, to admit or acknowledge, but the *ad-* is usually erased from *admettons que* in daily language.

faire (meaning to look, seem, or act like)

Faire is commonly used in this idiomatic sense, meaning to <u>appear</u>, to <u>seem</u>, to <u>act like</u>, to <u>look like</u>. For example:

> **Ne fais pas l'idiot !**
>
> Don't act like an idiot!
>
> **Il ne fait pas soixante ans.**
>
> He doesn't appear sixty years old. He doesn't seem sixty.
>
> **Elle ne fait pas son âge.**
>
> She doesn't show her age.
>
> **Elle fait plus jeune que son âge.**
>
> She seems younger than her age.

dont

Like *donc,* **dont** is one of the little words that lubricates the language and makes it flow. it means <u>of which</u> or <u>about which</u>. (It can also be translated <u>of</u>

whom or in which, but if you remember "of which" the other meanings will be self evident).

Les sujets dont je veux parler sont...

The subjects about which I want to talk are... / The subjects that I want to talk about are...

Il y a deux arbres dont l'un est un cerisier.

There are two trees, of which one is a cherry tree.

Il y avait six invités, dont Jacques faisait partie.

There were six guests, of which Jacques was one.

Et voici Marie, ma fille dont je suis si fier.

And here is Marie, my daughter of whom I am so proud.

Je n'aime pas la façon dont il me parle.

I don't like the way in which he talks to me / I don't like the way he talks to me.

au cas où...
à tout hasard

The expression *au cas où* means just in case. It is used frequently in spoken French, and in pretty much the same ways that we would use "just in case" in English.

> **Je vais prendre une veste, au cas où.**

>> I'll take a jacket, just in case.

> **Il faut être là, au cas où il arriverait ce soir.**

>> We should be there, in case he arrives this evening.

The expression **à tout hasard** is a synonym and also means <u>just in case</u>.

> **Je vais prendre une veste, à tout hasard.**

>> I'll take a jacket, just in case.

> **Il faut lui demandé, à tout hasard.**

>> We should ask him, just in case.

c'est pas la peine

C'est pas la peine is another very common expression in spoken French. It means <u>It's not worth the trouble</u> or <u>Don't bother</u>!

> **Je vais aller chercher encore du pain. --- C'est pas la peine. Nous en avons assez.**

>> I'll go get some more bread. --- It's not worth the trouble. We have enough of it.

C'est pas la peine d'aller à la boulangerie.
Nous en avons assez pour ce soir.

> It's not worth the trouble of going to the bakery. We have enough for this evening.

C'est pas la peine de lui demander. C'est sûr, il va refuser.

> It's not worth the trouble to ask him. It's certain that he will refuse.

Again, this is spoken French. if you are in a more formal situation, you have to say: *Ce n'est pas la peine* (reinserting the *n'*). In practice, what you'll hear is: *C'est pas la peine.*

haut de gamme
bas de gamme

La gamme is the range, of products, colors, articles, etc.

Haut de gamme means it's <u>top of the line</u>, <u>top quality</u>, top of the range.

Bas de gamme naturally means the opposite.

C'est un ordinateur haut de gamme.

> That computer is top quality.

Cette voiture est chère, mais c'est une voiture haut de gamme.

That car is expensive but it's a car which is top of the line.

C'est bon marché, mais c'est du bas de gamme.

It's cheap but it's poor quality.

C'est une émission bas de gamme.

It's an awful TV program.

à mon avis

The expression **à mon avis** is in constant use as it means in my opinion, and French people have opinions about nearly everything.

À mon avis, c'est stupide.

In my opinion, it's stupid.

Il n'arrivera pas à l'heure, à mon avis.

He won't come on time, in my opinion.

Naturally, you can also refer to notre avis, ton avis, votre avis, son avis, or leur avis when referring to other people.

Qu'est-ce qu'on doit faire, à ton avis ?

What should we do, in your opinion?

À son avis c'est Pierre qui l'a fait.

According to her opinion, it's Pierre who did it.

Il change d'avis comme de chemise.

He changes his opinions like his shirts.

à vrai dire

The expression **à vrai dire** means <u>to tell you the truth</u>, or <u>speaking frankly</u>. It usually precedes or follows some unpleasant truth.

Je m'en doutais, à vrai dire.

I suspected it, to tell the truth.

À vrai dire, je crains qu'il ne rate l'épreuve.

Frankly speaking, I fear that he is going to fail the test..

Since *rater* is a bit informal, in a more formal situation you'd say:

À vrai dire, je crains qu'il n'échoue à l'épreuve.

Although, as I said, *à vrai dire* is usually used with a negative thought, it can occasionally be used with a compliment.

À vrai dire, je la trouve assez belle.

To tell the truth, I find her pretty attractive.

Entendu !
Bien entendu !

Entendu literally means <u>Understood</u>! and is used
somewhat like *D'accord,* but there are nuances of
difference.

First of all, *Entendu* can mean that <u>something has</u>
<u>been explained to you and you have grasped it</u>:

Ce serait bien que tu sois là pour midi,
mais avant il faut que tu ailles à la bou-
langerie pour le pain et le dessert. --- En-
tendu !

It would be good if you could get there
by noon, but before that you have to go
by the bakery for the bread and the dessert.--- Understood!

Secondly, *Entendu* can mean that <u>something has</u>
<u>been discussed and decided and you are in agree-</u>
<u>ment</u>. After the discussion you can say:

Entendu !

Agreed! Decided!

C'est entendu !

It's agreed !

or more formally:

C'est une affaire entendue !

It's a deal. It's an agreed deal.

You can see how this differs from *D'accord*, which can be used in reply to a simple question like "Can you come for dinner tomorrow?" and means "Okay".

Finally, **bien entendu** means of course. It can be used alone as an exclamation, or included a sentence.

Vous serez là ? --- Bien entendu !

You'll be there? --- Of course!

Je suis arrivé à cinq heures mais, bien entendu, elle était partie à cinq heures moins le quart.

I had arrived at five o'clock, but of course, she had left at a quarter to five.

Et, bien entendu, je te paierai un bon prix.

And, of course, I will pay you a good price.

And let it be understood, I will pay you a good price.

quand même

The expression **quand même** means nevertheless,

<u>all the same</u>, <u>even so</u>, or <u>anyway</u>. You can use it pretty much whenever you would use one of these expressions in English.

Quand même, il aurait pu nous prévenir.

> *All the same, he could have let us know in advance.*

Il m'a déconseillé de m'éloigner. --- Vous êtes parti quand même ?

> He warned me not to leave. --- You left even so? / You left anyway?

Quand même, ça serait gentil de l'acheter pour elle en cadeau.

> Even so, it would be nice to buy it for her as a gift.

Il ne fait pas très froid maintenant, mais quand même je vais apporter une veste.

> It's not very cold right now, but even so I'm going to bring a jacket.

Tu as raison, ça monte très peu. Mais, ça monte quand même.

> You are right, it (the slope) goes up very gradually. But it's uphill all the same. (Heard bicycling).

When said as an exclamation, with a tone of humorous protest, it can be translated as <u>All the same</u>! or <u>Really</u>!

> *Je sais que tu as faim Jean Marc, mais quand même !*
>
>> I know you're hungry Jean Marc, but really! (aren't you overdoing it?).
>
> *Il fait froid, mais quand même, avec trois pulls tu exagères un peu !*
>
>> It's cold, but all the same, wearing three sweaters is a bit excessive / is a bit much!

tout de même

> *Tout de même* is a synonym for *quand même*. It means <u>all the same</u> and can be used pretty much the same way as *quand même*. *Quand même* is more common but both are used.
>
> *Tout de même, il aurait pu nous prévenir.*
>
>> *All the same, he could have let us know in advance.*

Tu exagères

> The verb *exagérer* can mean <u>to exaggerate</u> but it also often has an idiomatic meaning:
>
> *Tu exagères* (you are exaggerating) is used in ev-

43

eryday speech to say <u>That's a bit much</u>! or <u>That's a bit excessive</u>! or <u>You've got to be kidding</u>!

It implies that the person being addressed is doing something excessive and it suggests a bit of incredulity coupled with mild disapproval.

> *Je vais en acheter trois. --- Tu exagère un peu / Il ne faut pas exagérer*

> I'm going to buy three of them. --- You are going a bit overboard / Don't overdo it.

> *C'est son troisième dessert. --- Il exagère un peu.*

> It's his third dessert. --- He's being a bit excessive.

Tu exagères means "That's a bit excessive". It differs from "You are exaggerating" in ordinary English usage in two ways.

The first difference is that, in English, "you are exaggerating" means exclusively that you are <u>describing something unrealistically</u> as better, worse, bigger, smaller, etc than it really is. On the other hand, in French, *tu exagères* means that you are <u>being excessive</u> in what you are saying or doing.

The second difference is that, in English "you are exaggerating" is pretty much <u>restricted to speech</u>, while in French, *tu exagères* can refer to <u>excessive action and behavior as well as to speech</u>.

comme (meaning "as a")

Comme generally means <u>like</u> or <u>as</u>, and can be used in a number of senses. In the sense we will discuss here, it means <u>as a</u> in the sense of <u>in the role of</u>. The following examples should make it clear.

> **Elle travaille comme secrétaire.**
>
> > She is working <u>as a</u> secretary / <u>in the role of</u> secretary.

(Note that since *comme* here means "as <u>a</u>", the indefinite article *une* is not needed and is omitted before *secrétaire*).

> **Il était contremaître. Depuis qu'il a démissionné il travaille comme ouvrier.**
>
> > He was a foreman but since he quit he has been working <u>as a</u> common laborer.

> **Comme plombier il est nul, mais comme électricien il est excellent.**
>
> > <u>As a</u> plumber he's terrible but he's an excellent electrician.

> **Comme gérant, il est efficace.**
>
> > <u>As a</u> manager, he does a good job.

You'll remember that in these examples we used *comme* to mean <u>as a</u> to mean: <u>in the role of</u>.

On the other hand, you can use *comme* to simply

mean <u>as</u>. When you do, it has to be followed by *un* or *une*, as you'll see below.

> **Cette maison est grande comme un château.**

> That house is as big <u>as</u> a chateau.

> **Est-ce que je dois l'emballer comme un cadeau.**

> Should I wrap it <u>as</u> a present.

tout comme

Comme normally means like or as. **Tout comme** adds emphasis and means <u>just like</u> or <u>almost the same</u>.

You'll hear the expression *tout comme* fairly frequently. Synonyms would be *presque* and *presque pareil*.

> **Est-ce que le repas est prêt ? --- C'est tout comme.**

> Is the meal ready? --- It's just about.

> **Ton comportement est tout comme celui d'un bébé.**

> Your behavior is just like that of a baby. (Mother talking to a child)

> You are behaving like a baby.

Sa robe est tout comme la tienne.

Her dress is just like yours.

Her dress is exactly the same as yours.

comme il faut

This is another very common expression using *comme*.

Comme il faut can describe a place or person as an adjective phrase meaning <u>as it should be</u>, or <u>proper</u>.

Comme il faut can also modify a verb as an adverb phrase meaning is <u>as it should be</u> or <u>properly</u>.

Tout était comme il faut.

Everything was just as it should be.

C'est un restaurant comme il faut.

It's a restaurant that is just as it should be. (This is meant as a compliment).

Vous êtes habillé comme il faut.

You are dressed just right / just as you should be / very properly.

Ça se fait

This expression is very useful. **Ça se fait** says that

something is done, meaning that it's acceptable or proper to do it. The expression is usually used in the negative, as in :

Cela ne se fait pas.

That's not done. That's not acceptable behavior.

Or very casually, as:

Ça se fait pas !

That's not done!

Mâcher du chewing-gum ne se fait pas ici.

It's not proper to chew gum here.

Est-ce qu'on peut manger les côtes d'agneau avec les doigts ? --- Oui, Ça se fait.

Can one eat lamb chops with ones fingers? --- Yes. That's done / that's acceptable.

En Angleterre, les gens envoient avec la carte de Nöel une longue lettre pour raconter les évènements de l'année écoulée. Oui, ça se fait.

In England, people send a long letter with their Christmas card to recount all the events of the past year. Yes, that's done (acceptable).

ça se dit

The counterpart of *ça se fait* is **ça se dit**.

> **Est-ce qu'on peut dire cela en français ?**
> **--- Oui, ça se dit.**
>
> Can one say that in French? --- Yes. That can be said.

However, like *ça se fait*, *ça se dit* is used more often in the negative, as:

> **Cela ne se dit pas en bon français !**
>
> That's not said in good French!

More casually, it's *ça se dit pas,* as in :

> **Ça se dit pas ! C'est vulgaire.**
>
> One doesn't say that! It's vulgar.

à la rigueur
à la limite

À la rigueur and **à la limite** both mean <u>if worse comes to worst</u>, <u>in a pinch</u>, <u>if I have to</u>, <u>if I must</u>, <u>if it comes to that</u>, <u>if necessary</u>. They both imply "I don't really want to, but if I must, I must."

À la rigueur is stronger. It usually means that "I'll

do it if I <u>absolutely</u> have to". Theoretically, *à la limite* is a little milder and means something more like "I don't really want to but I'll do it if necessary". In practice though, it's hard to tell them apart and you can use them pretty interchangeably. For example:

> ***Je pourrais le faire, à la rigueur.***
>
> I would be able to do it, if necessary.
>
> ***À la rigueur, on peut trouver une autre solution.***
>
> In a pinch, we can find one another solution / If it comes to that, we can find another solution.
>
> ***C'est infect ! À la limite, je préfère ne rien manger que manger ça.***
>
> It's awful. If worse comes to worst, I'd rather eat nothing than eat that.

Tu parles !

The exclamation ***Tu parles !*** is very interesting because it can have two almost opposite meanings.

Ordinarily, *Tu parles !* is a sign of enthusiastic agreement, and means something like: <u>Dont I know it!</u> <u>You're telling me</u>? <u>That's for sure!</u> <u>I agree!</u>".

> ***S'il continue comme ça il va avoir des ennuis. --- Tu parles !***

If he continues like that, he's going to have problems. --- That's for sure!

Ah ! C'est une jolie femme. --- Tu parles !

Oh! She is an attractive woman. --- I agree! Don't I know it!

However, sometimes *Tu parles !* is said ironically and with a deprecatory tone of voice and means pretty much the opposite, something like: You've got to be kidding! You must be joking! You don't know what you're talking about!

Naturally, you should be able to tell by the tone of voice and the context.

Je crois qu'ils vont gagner la Coupe du monde. --- Oh, tu parles!

I think that they will win the World Cup. --- Oh, don't be silly!

aimer bien

As the French verb *aimer* can have two meanings with very different connotations, to like and to love, **aimer bien** is sometimes used to distinguish between them. When used in referring to a person, *aimer bien* means to like somebody a lot, or to really like somebody, but it **doesn't** mean to love the person. It thus avoids any chance of ambiguity.

Je l'aime bien.

I like him or her a lot.

Je l'aime.

More likely to mean I love him or her.

**Auparavant, je l'aimais bien, mais mainte-
nant je l'aime.**

Before I used to like him a lot as a friend,
but now I'm in love with him.

(This could also read: Before I used to
like her a lot as a friend, but now I'm in
love with her).

Side Note: *Aimer bien* can also refer to a thing or
an action, where it simply means to like it a lot. For
example: *J'aime bien cette maison* or *J'aime bien
manger le chocolat.*

Et alors ?

Et alors ? literally means <u>And then</u>? and is used
to say something like: <u>And so</u>? <u>And what of it</u>? <u>So
what</u>?

**Mais les voisins peuvent nous voir. --- Et
alors ?**

But the neighbors can see us. --- So
what! What of it?

Sometimes it's said with a touch a futility to say

There's not much we can do about it, or <u>What can we do about it</u>?

> ***Il est possible qu'ils aient triché. --- Et alors?*** (With a shrug of the shoulders)**.**
>
>> It's possible that they cheated. --- So, what can we do about it?

In other contexts *Et alors* can be said aggressively, as a challenge, meaning <u>So what are you going to do about it</u>?

> ***Vous êtes en train de danser avec ma copine. --- Et alors ?***
>
>> You're dancing with my girlfriend! --- And so, what are you going to do about it?
>
> ***Tu te soûle chaque soir ! --- Et alors ?***
>
>> You get drunk every evening! --- So what are you going to do about it?
>
> ***Tu n'as pas encore acheté du pain ! --- Et alors ?***
>
>> You haven't bought any bread yet! --- So what's the big deal?

au juste ?

Au juste means <u>exactly</u>. It's added to a question to request the person responding to be precise, (or more precise). This means that you can use it, and may hear it, in a multitude of circumstances. For example:

C'est où dans Paris, au juste?

It's where in Paris, exactly?

Quand est-ce que vous allez venir, au juste ?

When exactly are you going to arrive?

Ils étaient combien à la réunion, au juste ?

How many were at the meeting, exactly?

Ça coûte combien, au juste ?

How much exactly does that cost? / That costs how much, exactly?

Tu me dis de venir. Mais quand, au juste ?

You say I should come. But *when*, exactly?

Ça c'est fait comment, au juste ?

How exactly is that made?

Ça c'est quoi, au juste ?

What is that, exactly?

Remember that *au juste* is always used with one of

the question words *quand, combien, quoi, qui, comment* and *où.*

avoir l'habitude de
prendre l'habitude de
perdre l'habitude de

These three expressions mean: to have the habit of, to get in the habit of, to lose the habit of. As with most of the expressions in this book, they aren't restricted to any one circumstance but are very versatile.

They could also be translated: to be used to, to get used to, to no longer be used to. For example:

> **J'ai l'habitude de me coucher tard.**
>
>> I'm in the habit of going to bed late / I'm used to going to bed late.
>
> **J'ai pris l'habitude de me coucher tard quand j'étais étudiant.**
>
>> I got in the habit of going to bed late when I was a student.
>
> **Maintenant, j'ai perdu l'habitude de me coucher tard.**
>
>> Now, I've lost the habit of going to bed late / Now I'm not used to going to bed late.
>
> **J'ai l'habitude du froid.**

I'm used to cold weather.

J'ai l'habitude d'étudier pendant des heures.

I'm used to studying for hours at a time.

Nous avons perdu l'habitude de boire du vin pendant le repas.

We've gotten out of the habit of drinking wine with meals.

We're no longer used to drinking wine with meals.

dès que
sitôt

Dès que (the "s" is not pronounced), means <u>as soon as</u>. You can use *dès que* whenever you would say "as soon as" in English.

Il a commencé à travailler dès qu'il est arrivé.

He started to work as soon as he arrived.

Dès qu'il l'a vue, il a souri.

As soon as he saw her he smiled.

Another word meaning "as soon as" is **sitôt**. *Sitôt* is much less frequently used than *dès que*.

Il a commencé à travailler sitôt qu'il est ar-
rivé.

Sitôt arrivé, il a commencé à travailler.

en

The pronoun *en* can mean: <u>of it</u>, <u>of them</u>, <u>from it</u>, <u>from them</u>, <u>by it</u>, <u>because of it</u>, or <u>with it</u>. **It refers back to something**, or some things, **already mentioned**.

En has no counterpart in English but it is much used in spoken (and in written) French. I'm giving you a lot of examples to show some of the many different ways *en* is used:

> **Avez-vous des melons ? --- Combien en**
> **voulez-vous ? --- J'en veux quatre.**

> > Do you have melons? --- How many <u>of</u>
> > <u>them</u> do you want? --- I'd like four <u>of</u>
> > <u>them</u>.

Because it has no counterpart in English, English speakers tend to omit the *en* when speaking French. In the sentence above, they might just say *"Je veux quatre"* instead of *"J'en veux quatre"*. Unfortunately, however, *"Je veux quatre"* is incorrect and sounds incorrect to a francophone. Using it gives you away as a non-native French speaker.

> **J'en étais bouleversé.**

> > I was shaken <u>by it</u>.

J'en ai trois.

I have three <u>of them</u>.

Elle n'en dort plus la nuit.

She doesn't sleep any more at night <u>be-cause of it</u>.

Est-ce qu'il a encore la grippe. --- Non. Il en est guéri.

Does he still have the flu. --- No. He is cured <u>of it</u>.

Combien il y en a ? --- Il y en a six.

How many <u>of them</u> are there? --- There are six <u>of them</u>.

J'en ai eu assez.

I have had enough <u>of it</u> or <u>of them</u>. (When eating, for example).

Avez-vous besoin d'essence? --- J'en ai assez.

Do you need gasoline? --- I have enough <u>of it</u>.

Est-ce qu'il y a beaucoup de voitures sur cette route ? --- Il y en a trop.

Are there a lot of cars on that route? --- There are too many (<u>of them</u>).

Just remember to drop the *en* into your sentence when you are referring back to something which has already been mentioned. Here are a few more examples. Practice putting in the translations yourself.

> *Quand Jean-Michel en aura fini...*

> *Où puis-je trouver un boucher ? --- Il y en a un rue Florentin.*

> *Il en était convaincu.*

> *Elle avait besoin d'une robe de soir. Elle m'a demandé s'il était vrai que j'en louais.*

au fur et à mesure

The expression **au fur et à mesure** means something pretty close to <u>as one goes along</u>. It's used for something that you do in little bits, as you go.

> *Nous en discuterons au fur et à mesure durant notre promenade.*

> > We will discuss it (a bit at a time) as we go along during our walk / We will talk about it as we go…

> *Vous allez apprendre à parler le français, et vous apprendrez la grammaire au fur et à mesure.*

> > You'll learn to speak French, and you'll learn the grammar as you go.

Regardez ces dessins et passez-les moi au fur et à mesure.

Look at these drawings and pass them to me as you go.

gêner
déranger

Gêner is a verb that means <u>to be in the way</u>, <u>to block</u>, <u>to disturb</u>, or when discussing an action, <u>to interfere</u> with it. For example:

(On a curbside sign) *Stationnement gênant.*

Parking here is in the way, it interferes with traffic. (The sign may have a little picture of a tow truck for emphasis).

Cet arbre gêne la vue.

That tree blocks the view.

However, the expression that is important for you to learn is a little expression of *politesse* (politeness). It asks <u>if you are bothering</u>, or will be bothering, the person you are talking to. You use it to politely ask permission to do something.

In this usage, the verb *déranger* is a common synonym, perhaps even more common, and I'll give examples of both below.

Bonjour Marie. Je te gêne ? / Je te dérange ?

Hi Marie. Am I bothering you? Did I call at the wrong time? Are you busy?

Ça te gêne si je...? / Ça te dérange si je...?

Est-ce que ça te gêne si je...? / Est-ce que ça te dérange si je...?

Does it bother you if I...?

Ça te gênera si j'allume la télévision?/ Ça te dérangera si j'allume la télévision?

Will it bother you if I put on the television.

And more formally:

Est-ce que cela vous gênerait / dérangerait si nous venions un peu plus tard ou tôt ?

Would it bother you (be a problem for you) if we arrive a bit later or earlier?

A second meaning for the verb *gêner* is to <u>embarrass</u> or <u>make to feel awkward</u>:

Elle était gênée de le rencontrer encore une fois.

She was embarrassed (she felt awkward) to run into him once again.

Il était un peu gênant de faire l'amour quand mes parents étaient dans la maison.

It was a little embarrassing / awkward to make love with my parents in the house.

Side Note: This brings us to another expression that I'll throw in just for free: *sans-gêne*. Literally *sans-gêne* means "without embarrassment". In practice it can best be translated as: without shame, shameless, impudent, brazen.

Oh ! Il est vraiment sans-gêne !

Oh! He's really shameless!

chouette

Chouette (pronounced "shwette"), is a colloquial expression of approval, which means, depending on context: <u>excellent</u>, <u>great</u>, <u>beautiful</u>, <u>pretty</u>, <u>agreeable</u>, <u>attractive</u>, or *"sympa"*.

Chouette expresses enthusiasm and is usually said with enthusiasm and gusto. It's most often used by young people but, as with many youthful expressions, it has spread throughout the population.

C'est chouette !

It's super!

Je t'invite pour demain soir. --- Chouette !

I'm inviting you for tomorrow night. --- Swell! great!

C'est une chemise très chouette.

It's a really beautiful shirt.

C'est un chouette type.

He's very "sympa".

Elle était très chouette avec nous.

She was very nice and likeable with us.

C'était une chouette balade.

It was a very nice walk.

Maman me manque quand elle part en voyage, mais en même temps c'est chouette parce que je fait plein de trucs avec papa que maman n'aimerait pas.

I miss Mommy when she's on a trip, but at the same time it's neat because I do a lot of things with Daddy that Mommy wouldn't like. (Paraphrased from *Lignes de faille* by Nancy Huston)

Side Note: By the way, the noun *une chouette* is an owl, and is not immediately related to the adjective *chouette* that you just learned.

chic

Chic, which ordinarily means elegant, can be used in casual language in the same way as *chouette*, meaning excellent or *"sympa"*.

C'est un très chic type.

He's very "sympa".

Marie est une chic fille.

Marie is a great girl.

Elle a été très chic avec nous.

She has been very nice *(sympa)* with us.

Chic ! can also be used as an exclamation in the same way as *Chouette !*

Je t'invite pour demain soir. --- Chic alors !

I'm inviting you for tomorrow evening. --- Great!

My daughter tells me she would use *Chic !* more often than *Chouette !* to accept an invitation. In response to an invitation you can also just say one of the following:

Est-ce tu peux manger avec nous demain soir ?

Oui, volontiers ! – Yes, gladly!

Avec plasir ! – With pleasure!

D'accord, merci. – Okay, thank you.

Merci, c'est très gentil. – Thanks, it's very nice of you.

Génial !

Génial ! is another expression like *chouette* and *chic*, which means <u>Terrific</u>! or <u>Great idea</u>! in casual speech.

> **On peut y aller demain. --- Génial !**
>
> We can go tomorrow. --- Great idea!

en avoir marre
j'en ai marre

The expression **en avoir marre** is a strong expression which means <u>to be fed up (with it)</u>. It's usually used as **j'en ai marre**. It's certainly an expression that you may have need of from time to time. For example: *J'en ai marre d'étudier le français !*

It would be possible to say *nous en avons marre* or *ils en ont marre*, meaning <u>we are fed up</u> or <u>they are fed up</u>, but you'll hear these less frequently.

We recently discussed the use of *en* as a pronoun. *J'en ai marre* is another example of its use.

> **J'en ai marre ! or J'en ai marre de tout ça !**
>
> I'm fed up with that!
>
> **J'en ai marre de tes âneries !**
>
> I've had enough of your imbecilities!

There are several expressions in English which say

the same thing as "I'm fed up with that". For example:

I've had enough of that.

I'm sick and tired of that.

I've had it up to here with that.

There are several synonymous expressions in French as well. For example:

J'en ai par-dessus la tête de ça.

I've had it up to here with that.

(literally "over my head")

Elle en a ras-le-bol de son boulot.

She's sick and tired of her job.

(literally "her bowl is full to the brim")

J'en ai assez de ses caprices.

I've had enough of her tantrums / whims.

J'ai plein le dos de ses caprices.

(literally, "my back is loaded down with" or "I have a full load of")

Ça suffit ! or **Trop c'est trop !**

That's enough! Too much is too much!

These are all pretty much equivalent expressions and you can use whichever you like interchangeably. *J'en ai marre* and *Ça suffit* are probably the ones you'll hear the most often, though.

je m'en fiche
je m'en fous
je m'en balance
je me moque

This brings us to **je m'en fiche** which means in essence: <u>I don't care a hoot about it</u> or <u>I couldn't care less about it</u> or <u>I don't give a damn about it</u>. *Je m'en fiche* is often said a bit scornfully.

If you refer to a particular thing that you don't care about, you no longer need the *en* and you drop it. You therefore say *je <u>me</u> fiche de (quelque chose)* as in:

> **Je m'en fiche. or Je me fiche de ça.**
>
> > I don't care about that. I couldn't care less about it.
>
> **Je me fiche de ses problèmes.**
>
> > I don't care about his problems.
>
> **Je me fiche de la politique or La politique, je m'en fiche.**
>
> > I don't give a darn about politics. (In the

second sentence you are referring <u>back</u> to *la politique* so you say *je m'<u>en</u> fiche.*)

Je m'en fiche is of course from casual spoken language. You will hear it used frequently.

There are several other expressions which mean about the same thing as *je m'en fiche.* For example, **je m'en fous** and **je m'en balance** are also from casual spoken language and have the same meaning.

On the other hand, **je me moque de ça** is more refined and literary French, while also meaning the same thing. However *se moquer de* can also mean to make fun of or to mock and you could be misunderstood if you don't use it correctly.

It's thus probably safer to stick with *je m'en fiche* in ordinary conversation. *The verb ficher* also has different meanings, but the meanings of *je m'en fiche* and *je me fiche de ça* are clear and not ambiguous.

Ça m'est égal.

Je m'en fiche is a strong statement meaning "I don't give a damn". If you just want to say that you don't care one way or another about a subject or a decision, you can use **ça m'est égal** which means <u>it's all the same to me</u>. *Ça m'est égal* is proper French while *je m'en fiche* is more casual French.

Qu'est-ce que tu préfères, aller à la pizze-

ria ou au restaurant chinois ce soir ? ---
Ça m'est égal.

Which would you prefer, to go to the pizzeria or to the Chinese restaurant this evening? --- It's all the same to me.

soi

The prounoun **soi** means <u>oneself</u> (or, if you are talking about a particular person, <u>himself</u> or <u>herself</u>). *Soi* itself can be used in a number of useful expressions which I will illustrate below. Afterwards I'll discuss a number of derivative expressions. Let's start with *soi*, itself:

Il est bon de rentrer chez soi quand on est fatigué.

It's good to return to one's home when one is tired.

Il faut rester maître de soi.

It's important to keep self-control.

It's necessary to stay in control of oneself.

It's necessary to remain master of oneself.

Il faut avoir confiance en soi.

It's necessary to have confidence in oneself.

C'est chacun pour soi.

It's every man for himself.

en soi

En soi can be translated by <u>in itself</u> or <u>intrinsically</u> or <u>by it's very nature</u> or <u>by itself</u>. For example:

C'est suffisant en soi.

That's sufficient in itself / by itself.

Cette loi n'est pas mauvaise en soi, mais son application n'est pas facile.

That law isn't bad in itself, but to apply it is not easy.

Cette épreuve, en soi, était accablante.

That ordeal, in itself, was overwhelming.

soi-disant

Literally, *soi-disant* means "self-saying" or "self-claiming". It usually refers to a person, and would be translated colloquially as <u>self-styled</u>.

Calling something *soi-disant* implies skepticism on the speakers part. A French synonym would be *prétendu*.

For example:

Ce soi-disant plombier n'y connaît rien en plomberie.

That self-styled plumber knows nothing about plumbing.

Soi-disant can also refer to something which isn't what it's claimed to be, in which case it's translated as so-called.

La soi-disant princesse...

The self-proclaimed / so called princess.

Sous la dictature, le soi-disant système de lois n'était qu'illusion.

Under the dictatorship the so called system of law was only an illusion

cela va de soi
ça va de soi

Translated word for word, **cela va de soi** (or *ça va de soi)* means "that goes by itself". It can be translated as that's self evident, or that goes without saying.

Ça va de soi que nous allons payer les frais.

It goes without saying that we are going to pay the expenses.

Ça va de soi !

That goes without saying! Of course!

Cela ne va pas de soi.

That's not self-evident at all ("and I'm not at all sure it's true").

soi-même

Soi-même is our final expression using *soi*. It means <u>oneself</u>.

Dans ce gîte, on doit faire le ménage soi-même.

In that rental cottage one has to do one's own housekeeping.

C'est très difficile de se juger soi-même.

It's very difficult to evaluate oneself.

On a du mal à se chatouiller soi-même.

It's difficult to tickle yourself.

peu importe

The French verb *importer* has two meanings. The first is familiar to us. *Importer* can mean "to import" (goods into the country).

The second meaning though, is "to matter or to have importance".

(This is where the English adjective "important" comes from. It's the present participle of *importer*, and, therefore, means "mattering" or "having importance").

Thus **peu importe** means <u>it's of little importance</u> or <u>it matters little</u>. For example:

> **Pierre ne peut pas venir à la réunion. -- Peu importe.**
>
> > Pierre can't come to the meeting. --- It matters little. It doesn't matter.
>
> **Peu importe qu'il vienne ou pas.**
>
> > It's of little importance if he comes or not.
>
> **Est-ce que tu préfères manger dans un restaurant chinois ou italien ? --- Peu importe.**
>
> > Do you prefer to eat at a Chinese restaurant or an Italian? --- It's of little importance.

n'importe

N'importe is a very similar expression but it isn't exactly the same. *N'importe* means <u>no matter</u> or <u>it doesn't matter</u>. For example:

> **Tu peux venir à n'importe quelle heure. Je serai à la maison toute la journée.**
>
> > You can come at no matter what time (at

any time you like, whenever you like). I'll be at the house all day.

Tu préfères lequel ? --- N'importe.

Which do you prefer? --- It's not important. It doesn't matter. Either one.

Vous pouvez le poser n'importe où.

You can put it down anywhere.

Tu fais n'importe quoi et tu crois que je vais l'accepter.

You just do whatever you like and you think that I will accept it.

Tu peux m'acheter n'importe quelle glace. J'aime tous les parfums.

You can buy me whichever flavor of ice cream. I like them all.

Cela peut arriver n'importe quand à n'importe qui.

That could happen to anyone, any time. (Literally "no matter when to no matter who").

Je n'y suis pour rien

The expression **Je n'y suis pour rien** is a denial. It means I had nothing to do with it or It has nothing to do with me. (Translated word for word it means "I'm not there for anything").

For example, this quote from a *policier*:

> **Montale, j'y suis pour rien. Je te jure.**
>
> > Montale, I had nothing to do with it. I swear to you.

This expression could also be used in the second person or third person.

> **Les apparences sont contre lui, mais je crois qu'il n'y est pour rien.**
>
> > The circumstances are against him but I believe that he has nothing to do with it.

> **Les apparences sont contre vous, mais je crois que vous n'y êtes pour rien.**
>
> > The circumstances are against you but I believe that you have nothing to do with it.

enfin

The adverb **enfin** is a very common word which has a number of differently nuanced meanings.

1. *Enfin* can mean <u>at least</u> in the following sense:

> **J'ai vu ton frère. Enfin, je pense que c'était lui.**

I saw your brother. At least I think it was he.

C'est un vrai maître aux échecs. Enfin, il joue beaucoup mieux que moi.

He's a real chess master. At least he plays much better than me.

2. *Enfin* can mean <u>finally</u> or <u>at last</u>.

Je vous ai enfin retrouvé.

I found you again at last.

Vous voilà ! Enfin !

There you are! Finally!

3. *Enfin* can also mean <u>in brief</u> or <u>to sum up</u>. (French synonyms would be *bref*, or *en somme*.)

Il y avait chez moi ma mère, mon père, mes frères... enfin toute la famille.

There were, at my house, my mother, my father, my brothers... in brief, the whole family.

Enfin, c'était de la folie.

To sum up, it was craziness.

4. *Enfin* can sometimes be used as a synonym for *cependant* or *néanmoins* and translated as <u>however</u> or <u>nevertheless</u>

Je te déconseille de faire ça, enfin tu fais ce que tu veux.

I advise you not to do that. However, you do what you want.

5. Finally, *enfin* can express exasperation, as in:

Mais enfin ! Il ment ! C'est pas vrai !

Oh! He's lying! It's not true!

Mais enfin, je vous l'avais déjà dit !

But really! I already told you!

en effet
en fait, de fait
effectivement
réellement

The expression *en effet* means <u>indeed</u>, <u>actually</u>, <u>really</u>, <u>in actual fact</u>. That's a lot of definitions for you to decipher but you'll understand better with a few examples:

Oui, j'étais là cet été, en effet.

Yes, I was there this summer, as a matter of fact.

Yes I was really there this summer.

En effet, je pensais la même chose.

Actually I was thinking the same thing.

The expressions **effectivement, réellement, en fait** and **de fait** mean pretty much the same thing as *en effet :* <u>actually</u>, <u>really</u>, <u>as a matter of fact</u>, <u>in fact</u>.

> **Oui, j'étais là cet été, effectivement.**

>> Yes, I was there this summer, as a matter of fact.

> **Oui, j'étais là cet été, réellement.**

>> Yes I was really there this summer.

> **En fait, je peux venir demain.**

>> In fact, I can come tomorrow.

There is a small nuance of difference, however, between *en effet* and *en fait.* Look at the next three examples:

> **Il a estimé que ça allait coûter mille euros, et en effet c'était le prix exact.**

>> He estimated that it would cost a thousand euros, and actually that was the exact price.

> **Il a estimé que ça allait coûter mille euros. En fait ça a coûté mille cinq cents.**

>> He estimated that it would cost a thousand euros. In fact it cost fifteen hundred.

> **Il m'a dit que la maison était en bon état. En fait elle était délabrée.**

He told me the house was in good shape.
In fact, it was dilapidated.

Note how *en effet* is used to confirm (that it was *mille euros*) while *en fait* (in fact) is used to contradict, to say that **in fact** it was different.

pendant que
tandis que

The expression ***pendant que*** means <u>while</u> in the sense of <u>during the time that</u>.

> ***Pendant qu'elle était à Paris, elle a visité le Louvre.***

> > While she was in Paris, she visited the Louvre. (During the time that...)

On the other hand, ***tandis que*** means <u>while</u> in the sense of <u>whereas</u> or <u>while on the other hand</u>.

In other words, one person (or thing) was doing or being something <u>while on the other hand</u>, another person (or thing) was doing something different or acting in a different way.

While things are occurring at the same time, there is a sense that they are opposing actions or states of being.

> ***Il est riche, tandis que son frère est pauvre.***

He's rich, while / whereas his brother is poor.

Son frère est resté chez eux, tandis qu'elle est venue à Paris.

Her brother stayed at home, while she came to Paris. (Make note of the difference between this and the Paris example above which used *pendant que*).

Son frère est paresseux, tandis qu'il est travailleur.

His brother is lazy, whereas he's a hard worker.

toujours
depuis toujours
pour toujours

- **Toujours** means always.

    Est-ce que tu m'aimeras toujours ?

    Do you think that you will love me always?

    Il a toujours vécu ici / Il va toujours vivre ici.

    He has always lived here. / He will always live here.

- If you make it **depuis toujours** it is literally "since always". It puts it specifically <u>in the past</u> and provides emphasis. It translates more like <u>forever</u>. Note the difference between:

> ***J'ai toujours voulu un chat.***
>
> I've always wanted a cat.
>
> ***J'ai voulu un chat depuis toujours.***
>
> > I've wanted a cat forever / I've wanted a cat all my life.

- On the other hand, ***pour toujours*** literally is "for always" and it sounds almost redundant to an English speaker. Using *pour* is usually used to specify a particular amount of time as in *pour trois jours*, but in the case of *pour toujours*, it anchors the sentence firmly <u>in the future</u> and seems also to be used for emphasis. It can be translated as "forever" or "permanently" or "for good". Actually, <u>for good</u> is probably the best translation.

> ***Elle est guérie pour toujours.***
>
> She is cured for good.
>
> ***Elle va rester ici pour toujours.***
>
> She will stay here for good.

You can see from these two examples that the nuance of meaning of *pour toujours* is indeed different from that of a simple *toujours*, although the difference may be hard to put into precise words.

il n'empêche que
n'empêche

The verb *empêcher* means: to prevent, to hold back from doing, to impede.

When translated word for word, the expression *il n'empêche que...* means <u>it doesn't prevent that</u>....

Thus, when you use it in a figurative sense, *il n'empêche que* means <u>nevertheless</u> or <u>even so</u>.

> **Nous avons gagné la bataille. --- Il n'empêche que nous l'avons payé cher.**
>
> > We won the battle. --- Nevertheless we paid dearly.
>
> **Nous serons quatre à travailler. --- Il n'empêche que cela va être un gros boulot.**
>
> > There will be four of us working. --- Even so it will be a big job.

In very casual speech, the expression is often shortened to just *N'empêche.*

> **Nous serons quatre à travailler. --- N'empêche, c'est un gros boulot.**
>
> > There will be four of us working. --- Even so, it's a big job.

> **N'empêche, tu aurais pu téléphoner.**

Nevertheless, you could have telephoned.

Ne t'inquiète pas !
T'inquiète !

The adjective *inquiet* in French (literally "unquiet"), translates as worried, anxious, uneasy or unquiet.

While in English, we would not make unquiet or uneasy into a verb (to unquiet?), the French make *inquiet* into *inquiéter*. The verb *inquiéter* means, naturally enough, "to make uneasy or worried".

The reflexive form *s'inquiéter* thus means "to make yourself worried" or "to get worried" or "to worry yourself".

From which we finally arrive at the common expression **Ne t'inquiète pas !** which means: <u>Don't worry yourself!</u>, <u>Don't upset yourself!</u>, <u>No big deal!</u>

> **Ne t'inquiète pas ! Ce n'est pas important.**

> Don't worry, it's not important.

In casual spoken French, *Ne t'inquiète pas !* is often abbreviated to *T'inquiète pas !* and, most frequently, to just *T'inquiète !*

> **T'inquiète pas ! C'est pas important.**

> **T'inquiète ! C'est pas important.**

Don't worry, it's not important.

Ne te fais pas de souci
Ne t'en fais pas
T'en fait pas
Pas de souci

The expression **ne te fais pas de souci** literally means <u>don't make worry for yourself</u>, and it's pretty much a synonym for *ne t'inquiète pas*.

> **Ne te fais pas de souci ! Ce n'est pas important.**

Don't worry, it's not important.

Ne te fais pas de souci is very often abbreviated as **Ne t'en fais pas** (where *en* takes the place of *de souci),* and even more often in casual speech as **T'en fais pas**.

> **Ne t'en fais pas ! Ce n'est pas important.**

Don't worry, it's not important.

> **T'en fais pas ! C'est pas important.**

Don't worry, it's not important.

Ne te fais pas de souci is also sometimes abbreviated using just the last three words **Pas de souci !** and means <u>No worry</u> in the sense of <u>No problem</u>.

> **Est-ce que tu peux faire ça pour moi ? ---**
> **Pas de souci !**

Can you do that for me? --- No worry! /
No problem!

We'll discuss *Pas de souci !* at greater length later
on when we discuss *Pas de problème !*

Ne te casse pas la tête !
Te casse pas la tête !

Ne te casse pas la tête is another similar expression. It literally means "Don't break your head", and
can be translated as "Don't rack your brains" or <u>Don't
worry about it, it's not important</u>.

> *Je ne vois pas comment je pourrai venir
> demain. --- Ne te casse pas la tête ! Ce
> n'est pas important.*

>> I don't see how I can come tomorrow. ---
>> Don't worry about it. It's not important.

In casual spoken French it's heard more commonly
as *Te casse pas la tête !*

> *Je crois pas que je puisse venir demain.
> --- Te casse pas la tête. C'est pas impor-
> tant.*

>> I don't think I can come tomorrow. ---
>> Don't worry about it. It's not important.

You must remember that expressions like
T'inquiète ! and *Te casse pas la tête !* from **spoken
French**, are not standard French. When you are in

a situation when standard French is expected, you must use the proper longer forms.

The French almost all use the casual forms in everyday speech, but expect standard French in more formal situations. This even carries over to written French, where someone writing a casual note to a friend may well use a short form. In a business letter, however, he or she will certainly use the standard long form.

I don't mean to confuse you with these expressions from casual speech. I include them because that's the way people talk, and this book is about spoken French and everyday expressions.

embêtant
Tu m'embêtes !
emmerdant
chiant

The verb *embêter* means: to irritate, bother or annoy. **Embêtant** is <u>annoying</u>.

> *Tu es très embêtant !*

> You are very annoying.

Finally we have the common expression:

> *Tu m'embêtes !*

> You are really getting on my nerves.

The context where these would be used are a mother to an annoying child, a sibling to another, one roommate or friend to another, one spouse to another. (It can be used as a semi-pleasantry and usually doesn't express serious anger).

Emmerdant and **chiant** are vulgar and slangy equivalents to *embêtant*. I am including them so that you will recognize them but I would advise you against using *emmerdant* or *chiant* in conversation. One has to be very familiar with both the language and social customs to be sure of not offending.

Attention !
fais attention
faire attention
fais gaffe

Attention ! means <u>Watch out</u>! or <u>Be careful</u>! and is obviously useful to know.

You use **Fais attention** when you are telling someone to watch out or to be careful around a particular thing or person. (It's *"Faites attention"*, of course, if you are using the *vous* form to address the person or persons you are talking to). If it's not an imperative, you can just use **faire attention**.

Fais attention ! C'est un manipulateur.

Watch out! / Be careful! He's a manipulator.

Faites attention si vous passez par là pendant la nuit.

> Watch out if you go past there at night.

Fais attention à ses dents.

> Watch out for her teeth. (referring to a dog)

Fais attention à toi quand tu vas skier.

> Be careful of yourself when you go skiing.

Fais attention. Tu vas tomber !

> Watch out, you are going to fall!

Il faut faire attention. La pente est très raide.

> You need to be careful. The slope is very steep.

A synonym of *Fais attention* is ***Fais gaffe***.

Fais gaffe. Tu vas tomber !

> Watch out, you are going to fall!

> Be careful, you'll fall.

This is a bit of an an odd idiom since *une gaffe* is a boat hook, or in casual language, a blunder. Nonetheless, *Fais gaffe !* means watch out!

prêter attention à

On the other hand, **prêter attention** *à* means <u>to pay attention to</u>. It's easy to confuse with *faire attention* which we just discussed, but it doesn't mean the same thing.

> **Prête attention à ta mère !**

> Pay attention to your mother!

> **Prêtez attention à ses conseils. C'est une femme sensée.**

> Pay attention to her advice. She's a sensible woman.

Gare à toi !

Gare à toi also means <u>Watch out</u>! However, while *Attention !* or *Faites attention !* is usually a well intentioned alerting, *Gare à toi !* often means "Watch out!" in the sense of a menace, as in:

> **Gare à toi si tu fais ça encore une fois!**

> You better watch out if you do that again!

In other cases *Gare à...* can mean "watch out for", just like *Attention à...*

> **Gare à cette marche qui n'est pas bien fixée.**

> Watch out for that loose step.

Gare à Jean-Luc !

Watch out for Jean-Luc!

voilà

In general, **voilà** means there's as in

Voilà ma maison ! - There's my house!

Voilà Jean ! - There's Jean!

Le voilà ! means "There he is!" or "There it is!" but it can also mean "Here he is!" or "Here it is!"

Te voilà ! - There you are!

La voilà ! - Here she is!

Me voilà ! - Here I am!

Notice that you use the direct objects *Le, La, Te* or *Me* and not the subjects *Il, Elle, Tu* or *Je,* with these expressions.

People may also say *Voilà* when they hand you something (a package in a store for instance).

Voilà vos pommes. – Here are your apples.

Voilà ! – Here it is! / Here they are!

Next I have four expressions which you are more likely to encounter in reading rather than in conversation, but which can be very confusing. They are *quitte à, avoir beau, se garder de faire,* and *qui fait.*

quitte à

The expression **quitte à** has the sense <u>even if it means</u> or <u>even at the risk of</u>.

Starting from *"quitte à"*, this meaning is very unintuitive for an English speaker, so you may be led astray. Here are some examples:

> **Je finirai ce travail, quitte à revenir demain matin.**
>
> > I'll finish the job, even if it means coming back tomorrow morning.
>
> **Je resterai avec toi jusqu'au bout, quitte à mourir ensemble.**
>
> > I'll stay with you to the end, even if it means dying together.

avoir beau

The expression **avoir beau** is another very unintuitive little idiom. *Avoir beau* means: <u>even though</u>, <u>inspite of</u>, <u>no matter how hard</u>.

A French synonym would be *bien que* but the sentence structure is different. Avoir beau is usually used in the form: *J'ai beau (with the verb in the **infinitive**), je (with the second verb in the **present** tense)*. I know that this makes no sense at all without some examples, so here they are:

> **J'ai beau essayer, je n'y arrive pas.**

Even though I try / Inspite of trying / No matter how hard I try, I don't succeed.

Elle a beau lui expliquer, il ne comprend pas.

Even though she explains to him, he doesn't understand.

Il a beau le lui dire, elle ne veut rien entendre.

No matter how hard he tries to tell her, she just won't listen.

Even though he tells her, she doesn't want to hear.

Even though the expression starts with a *"j'ai"* or an *"il a"* you actually do use it with the infinitive instead of the past participle, and you do translate it in the present tense. It's very peculiar, but that's the way it is.

If you want to use *avoir beau* in the past you'd say: *j'avais beau... (keeping the verb in the infinitive), je... (with the second verb in the imparfait to match the "avais").*

J'avais beau essayer, je le ratais à chaque fois.

Even though I tried / Inspite of having tried / No matter how hard I tried, I failed every time.

Elle avait beau lui expliquer, il ne comprenait pas.

Even though she explained, he didn't understand.

Il avait beau se dire qu'elle allait venir, il savait bien que ce n'était pas le cas.

No matter how hard he told himself that she would come, he knew very well that it wouldn't happen.

se garder de (faire quelque chose)

The expression *se garder de*, when followed by an infinitive, means <u>to be careful not to do</u> or <u>to be careful to avoid doing</u>.

Although *se garder de* expresses a negative, you don't have to include a *ne...pas* with the verb that comes after it to make it negative. This probably sounds confusing too so here are some examples:

Il s'est bien gardé de donner la vraie raison de sa visite.

He was very careful <u>not to give</u> the true reason for his visit / He was careful <u>to avoid giving</u> the true reason...

(It says he was careful <u>not to give</u>, but there is no *ne...pas*. The *se garder de* takes care of that by itself.)

Il se garde de manger les huîtres crues.

> He is careful not to eat raw oysters / He is careful to avoid eating…

Il se garde bien de déposer tout son argent à la banque.

> He is careful not to deposit all his money at the bank.

Je m'en garderai bien.

> I'll be careful not to do that. / Don't worry! No way I'll do that!

Gardez-vous de vendre l'héritage.

> Be careful not to sell the heritage. Don't sell the farm. (Dying father to kids).

Note that, on the other hand, when the expression *se garder* is followed by the name of a food, instead of a verb, it means <u>to keep well</u>. It's a different meaning entirely. For example:

Le poisson se garde au réfrigérateur.

> Fish keeps well in the refrigerator.

Les ailes de raie ne se gardent pas bien. Elles sont fragiles.

> Skate wings don't keep well. They're fragile (and spoil easily).

Also when *se garder de* is followed by a person or a

thing it means <u>guard yourself from</u>, <u>watch out for</u> or <u>don't trust</u> or <u>be on the guard for</u>. For example:

Il faut se garder des flatteurs .

Garde-toi de Philippe.

qui fait (quelque chose)

This expression isn't quite so unintuitive. It refers to someone or something who is <u>in the act of</u>, or <u>in the process of</u>, doing something. It can be used with any verb, not just with *faire*.

It's the sentence structure, which is unusual for us anglophones, which makes *qui fait* idiomatic for us.

Je l'entends dans la cuisine, qui fait le petit déjeuner.

> I hear her in the kitchen, in the act of making breakfast.

Je l'ai vu dans le salon, qui étudiait fort.

> I saw her in the living room, studying hard / in the act of studying hard.

J'ai vu Jean dans sa chambre, qui se reposait enfin.

> I saw Jean in his room, resting at last / in the process of resting at long last.

I have heard each of these last four idioms used in

spoken language not infrequently but you are probably even more likely to encounter them in reading.

en fin de compte
tout compte fait
au bout de compte

The expression **en fin de compte** is translated as <u>when you sum it all up</u> or <u>to conclude</u> or <u>in conclusion</u>.

Although *en fin de compte* is similar to the expression *enfin* which was discussed earlier, and could possibly be used as a synonym for it, *en fin de compte* is stronger and more encompassing than *enfin*.

Enfin is usually used simply to sum up the speakers words as in:

> *Il y avait ma mère, mes frères... enfin toute la famille.*

> *Enfin, c'était stupide.*

En fin de compte, on the other hand, is more likely to be used after a discussion to sum up what has been decided. It expresses a conclusion. For example:

> (after a discussion) - *En fin de compte, il paraît que nous avons un grave problème ici.*

To sum up, it appears that we have a serious problem here.

If you compare the above examples, the difference in usage between *enfin* and *en fin de compte* should become clear.

Tout compte fait and **au bout de compte** are synonyms of *en fin de compte*. They are probably less common. Pick *en fin de compte* to add to your active vocabulary and just add the others to the expressions which you can recognize if you encounter them.

> **Tout compte fait, il paraît que nous avons un grave problème ici.**

> **Au bout de compte, il paraît que nous avons un grave problème ici.**

vos coordonnées

You will frequently be asked for **vos coordonées**, which means your <u>address, phone number, email address, etc</u>.

> **Donnez-moi vos coordonnées s'il vous plaît.**

> Give me your address and phone number, please.

> **Est-ce que vous pouvez me donnez vos coordonnées?**

Can you give me your address and phone number?

par la suite
ensuite

While the <u>adjective</u> "next" is translated by *prochain* or *suivant*, as in *la semaine prochaine*, the <u>adverb</u> "next" can be translated by ***par la suite*** as in:

> ***Et qu'est-ce qu'ils ont fait par la suite ?***

> And what did they do next?

> ***Qu'est-ce que je dois faire par la suite ?***

> What should I do next?

> ***Par la suite, j'ai rendu visite à Jean.***

> Next, I visited Jean.

Other terms that you can use for the same purpose are ***ensuite*** and *après cela*. For example:

> ***Ensuite, j'ai rendu visite à Jean.***

> ***Après cela j'ai rendu visite à Jean.***

tout à l'heure

The expression ***tout à l'heure*** is rather unique as it can mean either <u>a little while ago</u> or <u>in a little while</u>. *Tout à l'heure* is a very common expression:

À tout à l'heure !

I'll see you in a little while.

Il est arrivé tout à l'heure.

He arrived a couple of minutes ago.

Je vais rentrer tout à l'heure.

I'll be back in a few minutes.

Ça m'étonnerait (que)

As you know, I've been attempting to give you expressions which are not resticted to one specific circumstance but which can be used every day, or nearly every day. ***Ça m'étonnerait que...*** is one of those expressions. It can be translated as <u>It would surprise me if</u> or <u>I'd be surprised if</u>. You can be surprised about anything you want.

Surprendre is the verb which is closest in stem to "to surprise" and *étonner* is closer to "to astonish", but you will almost never hear *Ça me surprendrait* to mean "That would surprise me" In normal usage. It's place has been taken by *Ça m'étonnerait*.

Ça m'étonnerait qu'elle arrive demain.

It would surprise me if she comes tomorrow.

I'd be surprised if she comes tomorrow.

Ça m'étonnerait qu'elle soit une vraie blonde.

> It would surprise me if she's a real blond.

Il dit qu'il peut le faire. --- Ça m'étonnerait !

> He says that he can do it. --- That would surprise me! (ironic)

The negative of this expression, *Ça ne m'étonnerait pas*, is also commonly used to say It wouldn't surprise me.

Ça m'étonnerait pas qu'elle ait beaucoup souffert avec ce mari là.

> I wouldn't be surprised if she has suffered a lot with that husband of hers.

Ça ne m'étonnerait pas qu'elle arrive demain.

> It wouldn't surprise me if she comes tomorrow.

> I wouldn't be surprised if she comes tomorrow.

Just as in English, putting the negative on the second verb instead of on *étonnerait* changes the meaning.

Ça m'étonnerait qu'elle n'arrive pas demain.

It would surprise me if she doesn't come tomorrow.

The expression can also be used in the simple present tense as in:

Elle n'est pas ici ? Ça m'étonne.

She's not here?. That surprises me.

Ça ne m'étonne pas vraiment.

That doesn't really surprise me.

je n'en reviens pas

Translated word for word, *Je n'en reviens pas* means something like "I am not coming back to it" or "I'm not coming back from it". However, the fluent translation is <u>I can't get over it</u> when you are emotionally moved, and <u>I can't believe it</u> when you are astonished.

Here are some examples:

Je n'en reviens pas qu'il soit mort.

I can't get over it that he's dead.

Il n'en revenait pas.

He didn't get over it.

Je n'en reviens toujours pas, tu sais, murmura Harry, l'oeil embué de larmes.

I still can't get over it, you know, mur-
mured Harry, his eyes filling with tears.

**Elle n'en revient pas de l'avoir vu si mal-
ade.**

She can't get over having seen him so
sick.

**Nous avons vraiment réussi ? Je n'en re-
viens pas !**

We really did it? I'm astonished!

We really did it? I can't believe it!

ainsi que

The word *ainsi* means "thus" as in:

**Ainsi a fini notre troisième journée sur
l'île.**

and the two words *ainsi* and *que,* when put together
as separate words, mean "thus that" as in:

C'est ainsi qu'elle est arrivée ici.

It is thus that she arrived here.

**C'est ainsi que se termine ce roman,
avec...**

It's thus that this novel ends, with...

Ainsi que j'ai déjà expliqué...

Thus that / As I have already explained...

However, when *ainsi que* is put together as an expression it means <u>as well as</u>.

Je le connais déjà, ainsi que son frère.

I know him already, and his brother as well.

Il peut parler anglais ainsi que allemand et français.

He can speak English as well as German and French.

Ils élèvent des chèvres ainsi que des brebis.

They raise goats as well as sheep.

franchement

Franchement is another useful multi-purpose word. Most commonly, *franchement* means <u>frankly</u>, <u>openly</u>, <u>sincerely</u>, <u>honestly</u>. Here are some examples:

Je te dis franchement ce que j'en pense.

I'm telling you frankly what I think about it.

Franchement, je ne sais pas quoi faire.

Frankly, I don't know what to do.

Je vais te parler franchement.

I'm going to speak frankly.

As an exclamation, *Franchement !* expresses impatience or annoyance. It still means frankly speaking but can also be translated as Really, now! or something similar, as in:

Franchement ! Tu exagères !

Really now! You are going too far!

Tu es bête, franchement !

You're really stupid!

You're being stupid, to speak frankly! / You're being stupid, to tell the truth!

Franchement should not be confused with *forcément* or *vachement* which will be the next two terms I'll discuss.

forcément

The word **forcément** literally means "forcedly", and in practice can be translated by: of course, inevitably, necessarily, obviously, or obligatorily. Consider the following:

Il y avait un gros bouchon sur la route et nous étions forcément en retard.

There was a large traffic jam on the road and we were, of course, late.

*Elle sera forcément triste quand elle en-
tendra les nouvelles.*

> She will inevitably be sad when she hears
> the news.

> It's sure / It's certain that she will be sad
> when she hears the news.

When used by itself as an exclamation, **Forcément !**
means Of course!

A French synonym would be *Bien sûr !*

Tu seras là demain ? --- Forcément !

> You'll be there tomorrow? --- Of course!
> *(Bien sûr !)*

Finally, **pas forcément** means not necessarily, as
in:

*Ce n'est pas forcément une très bonne
idée.*

> That's not necessarily a great idea.

vachement

The adverb *vachement* is very slangy and not to be
used at all except in very informal situations. It is
used to intensify, and means "to a very high degree".
It has nothing to do with a cow *(une vache)*

Vachement can be translated as fantastically or
damned or really. French synonyms would be *drôle-*

ment or *rudement*. *Vachement* is usually a positive admiring expression as in:

Elle a vachement bien réussi.

She has succeeded fantastically well.

C'est vachement bien.

It's damned good.

La soupe est vachement bonne.

The soup is fantastically delicious.

However, occasionally *vachement* will accentuate a negative as in:

Il pleut vachement !

It's really raining!

Je suis vachement embêté.

I'm really bothered. (I can't find the answer to the problem).

Il est vachement con.

He is damned stupid.

You can almost always tell whether it is accentuating the positive or the negative from context.

à l'insu de

The expression **à l'insu de** means <u>without the knowl-</u>

edge of. It's another nice expression which can be used in many situations.

> **Il a acheté ça à l'insu de sa femme.**
>
> > He bought that without his wife's knowledge.
>
> **Elle l'a fait à l'insu de Pierre.**
>
> > She did it without Pierre's knowledge / behind Pierre"s back.
>
> **à mon insu**
>
> > without my knowledge / behind my back
>
> **à son insu**
>
> > without his (her) knowledge
>
> **à leur insu, à notre insu**

Side Note: When I first encountered *à l'insu de* I thought that it was a very peculiar expression which made no sense. Since, I have realized that *su* is the past participle of *savoir* (to know). Thus, as an adjective *su* means "known", and as a noun, *le su* is "the knowledge". Thus *l'insu* is "the lack of knowledge"! *L'insu* is only used in this expression.

étant donné que

> **Étant donné que** is a very useful and easy to remember expression. Word for word it means "being

given that", and <u>given that</u> is exactly what it actually means.

You could also translate *étant donné que* as <u>considering that</u> or <u>in view of</u> or even simply as <u>since</u> or <u>because</u>. It's used to say that in light of one thing happening, another is considered or possible. It's used in expressions like:

> *Étant donné que tu es très fatigué, nous devrions peut-être rester chez nous ce soir.*

>> Given that you are very tired, maybe we should stay home tonight.

> *Étant donné qu'on ne peut pas réserver, il est préférable d'arriver tôt.*

>> Given that we can't make a reservation, it will be better to arrive early.

> *Étant donné qu'il n'est pas arrivé, il faut modifier notre plan.*

>> Since he hasn't arrived, we have to change our plan.

> *Étant donné que le vol est annulé, nous devons nous y rendre en voiture.*

>> Given that the flight is cancelled, we have to get there by car.

> *Étant donné qu'il travaille à la mairie, il doit être au courant.*

Given that / since he works at the town hall, he should be in the know / he should know what's going on.

You can reverse the order of the sentence without any problem:

Il doit être au courant, étant donné qu'il travaille à la mairie.

He ought to know what's going on since he works at the town hall / given that he works at the town hall.

Étant donné que gives you one of those rare chances to use an expression which sounds right in English and, amazingly, sounds just right in French as well.

puisque
du moment que

Puisque means <u>since</u> or <u>seeing that</u>, and thus is a synonym for *étant donné que :*

Puisqu'il travaille à la mairie, il doit être au courant.

Another synonym for *étant donné que* is **du moment que**. This makes less sense to an anglophone, since if we were to translate it word for word it says something like "from the moment that". However, *du moment que* does indeed mean <u>given that</u>, <u>because</u>, or <u>since</u>.

Elle est heureuse, du moment qu'il y a beaucoup à manger

> She's happy, given that there's plenty to eat.

Du moment qu'il n'est pas arrivé, il faut modifier notre plan.

> Given that he hasn't arrived / Since he hasn't arrived, we need to modify our plan.

Du moment que is used fairly often. However, it's such an unintuitive way to say "given that" for an anglophone that you are less likely to actually use it yourself. You need to be able to recognize it though, as you will certainly encounter it in reading.

Side Note: In English, we use the same word, "since", for two entirely different meanings, which have to be translated differently into French.

The **first** meaning of "since" is "given that" or "because". This sense is translated into French by *étant donné que*, by *puisque*, or by *du moment où*.

Étant donné que l'avion est en retard...

> Since the plane is late... (given that)

The **second** meaning of "since" in English refers to an intervening period of time, and is translated in French by *depuis*.

Je ne l'ai pas vu depuis que je suis arrivé.

110

I haven't seen him since I arrived. (in the time intervening)

If you think about these two different meanings for the English word "since" you'll realize that they are totally different. These meanings aren't related to each other at all.

compte tenu de
vu que
parce que
comme

This is a group of French expressions which all can mean roughly about the same thing as *étant donné que* and *puisque*. They are **compte tenu de** or **compte tenu que** (taking into account that), **vu que** (seeing that), **comme** (as), and **parce que** (because).

> **Compte tenu qu'il n'est pas arrivé, il faut...**

> **Vu qu'il n'est pas arrivé, il faut...**

> **Parce qu'il n'est pas arrivé, il faut...**

> **Comme il n'est pas arrivé, il faut...**

> **Compte tenu de l'annulation du vol, nous devons nous y rendre en voiture.**

d'après...
selon

The expression *d'après* is very simple. It means <u>according to</u>:

> **D'après Jean, il va neiger demain.**
>
>> According to Jean it's going to snow tomorrow.
>
> **D'après Marie Claire, Evelyne va arriver à l'aéroport à cinq heures.**
>
>> According to Marie Claire, Evelyne will arrive at the airport at five o'clock.

You can reverse the order without problem:

> **Il va neiger demain d'après Jean.**
>
>> It's going to snow tomorrow according to Jean.

A French synonym for *d'après* is **selon:**

> **Selon Jean il va neiger demain.**

être pris

Literally, *je suis pris* means <u>I am taken</u>, and it's the term you use when you are invited out, but you already have plans:

> **Oh, dommage ! Je suis pris samedi soir.**

Oh, what a shame! I'm busy Saturday evening.

Je suis désolé, mais nous sommes pris mardi. Est-ce que jeudi vous convient?

I'm very sorry, but we already have plans for Tuesday. Would Thursday work for you?

tenir pour acquis

The expression **tenir pour acquis** means to consider as already established. You could also translate it as to take for granted. You can use it whenever you would say that something was taken for granted.

Il a tenu pour acquis qu'il allait gagner. C'était une grave erreur.

He took it for granted that he was going to win. It was a serious error.

Il a tenu les premiers trois axiomes pour acquis.

He considered the first three axioms as already established and not needing proof.

It's the *acquis* that counts. If you forget *tenir pour acquis* you can say *considéré comme acquis* and it will do just fine:

Nous pouvons considérer comme acquis ce premier point.

We can take for granted that there's agreement on the first point.

We can consider the first point as already established.

par erreur

The term **par erreur** is fairly self evident but it's useful, frequently used, and important to know. It means, naturally enough <u>by error</u>, <u>in error</u>, <u>by mistake</u>.

Pardon, j'ai ouvert cette porte par erreur.

Pardon me, I opened this door in error.

Je crois qu'elle l'a fait par erreur.

I believe she did it by mistake.

par mégarde

The term **par mégarde** is similar to *par erreur* but has a different shade of meaning. It means <u>accidently</u>, <u>inadvertently</u>, <u>not on purpose</u>.

The trick I've used to remember it is to think of *regarder* "to look at" and then think of *par mégarde* as "by not looking at" or "by inattention".

A friend subsequently pointed out that *par mégarde* actually comes from *mal garder* or the action of *ne pas prendre garde* (to not be on ones guard). Either way, *par mégarde* means "by inattention".

> **Elle a renversé la petite table par mégarde.**
>
>> She knocked over the little table accidently.
>>
>> She knocked over the little table by not paying attention.
>
> **Je l'ai laissé à la maison par mégarde.**
>
>> I left it at the house accidently.

Side Note: As you can see, *par erreur* and *par mégarde* can overlap but they actually do have somewhat different meanings. If you said *Elle a renversé la table par erreur* it could imply that she meant to knock over something else instead, or a different table . If you say that she did it *par mégarde* it's clear that it was by accident and inattention.

doucement
en douce

> The adverb ***doucement*** means: <u>softly</u>, <u>slowly</u>, <u>gently</u>, <u>carefully</u>. Consider these examples:
>
> **Parlez plus doucement, s'il vous plaît.**
>
>> Please speak more slowly (or softly, depending on context).

Nous avons marché doucement pour ne pas faire de bruit.

We walked softly so as not to make any noise.

Il a frappé doucement à la porte.

He knocked softly / gently at the door.

Elle ouvre la porte et elle entre doucement.

She opens the door and enters quietly.

Doucement, les enfants !!!!

Quiet down, kids !

La route descend doucement.

The route descends gradually.

You will use *doucement* often, especially in asking people to talk more slowly. *Lentement* would serve the same purpose, but French people use *doucement*.

Parlez plus doucement s'il vous plaît. Je (ne) peux pas comprendre.

On the other hand, the term ***en douce*** also means <u>quietly</u> but has the connotation of <u>discretely</u>, and even <u>furtively</u>, <u>secretly</u> or <u>on the sly</u>.

Elle est partie en douce quand il est arrivé.

She slipped away quietly when he arrived.

Elle a continué à lui donner de l'argent en douce.

She continued to give him money on the sly / discretely.

Elle se mit à rire en douce.

She started to laugh furtively.

Il a fait un coup en douce.

He played a sneaky trick.

il vaut mieux

If you translate it word for word **il vaut mieux** says "it's worth better". In practice you'd translate it as <u>it's better to</u>. You can put any verb after it that you like.

Il vaut mieux is another expression which can be used in a large variety of different circumstances.

Il vaut mieux refuser.

It's better to refuse.

Il vaut mieux arriver tôt.

It's better to arrive early.

The above sentences are built with the infinitive of the next verb *(refuser, arriver)*. However, if you structure the sentence *il vaut mieux **que...*** you use the subjunctive of the following verb.

> *il vaut mieux que tu refuses / que vous refusiez.*
>
> > It's better that you refuse.
>
> *Il vaut mieux que nous arrivions tôt.*
>
> > It's better that we arrive early.

You can also say "It <u>would</u> be better" by using the conditional, saying: *il <u>vaudrait</u> mieux.* For example:

> *Il vaudrait mieux rester.*
>
> > It would be better to stay.
>
> *Il vaudrait mieux que nous ne venions pas.*
>
> > It would be better if we didn't come / We had better not come.

manquer

Manquer (<u>to miss</u>) is a difficult verb for English speakers to get a feel for. This is due primarily to the odd structure (odd to us, that is), of the sentences in which *manquer* is used.

If the phrase starts *il manque (with an noun)* it translates one way:

> *Il manque deux tasses.*

Two cups are missing.

Il manque un bouton à ta chemise.

A button is missing off your shirt

Il manque Marie.

Marie is missing. Marie isn't here.

If you start with a noun it translates differently.

Marie me manque beaucoup.

I miss Marie a lot.

Notice the difference between **Il manque Marie** and **Marie me manque.** The first means "Marie is missing", the second means "I miss Marie". They are totally different.

You have to think of **Marie me manque** as "Marie is missing to me", and then translate it to yourself into vernacular English. Since this is how you say that you miss someone in French, you have to learn it. Here are some more examples to help out:

Marie nous manque.

We miss Marie.

Ma maison me manque / Mon chien me manque.

I miss my house / I miss my dog.

Ses chats lui manquent.

He misses his cats.

Finally, note that *manquer* (to miss) can be used in the same sense as the English word "miss" when you talk about missing a train or a flight.

> ***J'ai manqué le train.***
>
> > I missed the train. (*J'ai manqué le départ du train* is understood. A French synonym would be *J'ai raté le train)*.

Side Note: It's interesting that in English, "to miss" can have three different meanings: He is missing (not here), I miss him (remember him fondly), I missed my flight (didn't arrive on time), and that *manquer* in French can have all three of the same meanings.

Il y a quelque chose qui cloche (là-dedans)

> The rather picturesque expression *Il y a quelque chose qui cloche* means that while at first glance an idea, a plan, a proposal, a deal, etc, <u>appears</u> okay, you feel, intuit or <u>suspect</u> that <u>there is something wrong</u>. You may not quite be able to put your finger on it, but you sense it.
>
> *Il y a quelque chose qui cloche* can be translated by a variety of vernacular English expressions. For example:
>
> > ***Il y a quelque chose qui cloche dans cette affaire.***

There is something that's not quite right with this business.

There is something wrong with this.

There's something about this that doesn't add up.

There is something phony about this deal.

C'est une idée / un plan / une proposition intéressante mais il y a quelque chose qui cloche.

It's an interesting idea / plan / proposition but there is something wrong / something which doesn't sit right / something which doesn't quite add up / something which doesn't quite fit.

louche
il y a quelque chose de louche (là-dedans)

While *il ya quelque chose qui cloche là-dedans* means that there's something that's not quite right in that plan, idea, proposal, etc, ***il y a quelque chose de louche là-dedans*** means that there is something crooked, fishy, shady, suspicious or dubious about the subject at hand.

Il y a quelque chose de louche dans son passé.

There is something suspicious / something crooked in his past.

Il y a quelque chose de louche dans ces affaires.

There is something shady about those matters.

Il y a quelque chose de louche dans cet homme.

There's something suspicious about that man.

Note that each of these sentences could be worded more briefly, with the same ultimate meaning. For example:

Il a un passé louche.

Ce sont des affaires louches.

C'est un homme louche.

pour ainsi dire

The expression *pour ainsi dire* translated word for word would be "for thus to speak". In practice it's translated <u>so to speak</u>. You can use it whenever you would say "so to speak" in English.

J'admets que j'ai parlé un peu hâtivement, mais c'est ma nature, pour ainsi dire.

I admit that I spoke a bit hastily, but it's my nature, so to speak.

Elle pouvait happer au passage, pour ainsi dire, les regards d'autrui.

She could snatch on the fly, so to speak, the regards of others. (This example and the previous one are paraphrased from Les Thibault by Roger Martin du Gard. The latter especially is rather poetic and literary.)

Il a volé mon idée, pour ainsi dire.

He stole my idea, so to speak.

Jean a disparu dans la nature, pour ainsi dire.

Jean dropped out of sight, so to speak.

à peine
ne...guère

The two expressions *à peine* and *ne...guère* are closely related and are almost synonyms.

À peine means <u>hardly</u>, <u>scarcely</u>, <u>barely</u>, *<u>presque pas</u>*, *<u>très peu</u>*.

ne...guère means <u>hardly any</u>, <u>not much</u>, <u>not many</u>, <u>not very</u>, *<u>pas beaucoup</u>*, *<u>pas très</u>*.

I included the French synonyms above as they

seemed to differentiate between the meanings better than the English translations, but it may still sound as if *à peine* and *ne...guère* mean about the same thing. Well, actually they do mean about the same thing, but their usage can be different in a few cases. Here are some examples to help illustrate. We'll start with *à peine* :

> **C'était à peine visible.**

> It was scarcely visible.

> **Il arrive à peine.**

> He's hardly / barely / just arrived

> **il peut à peine marcher.**

> He can barely walk.

> **J'ai à peine vingt euros.**

> I have barely twenty euros.

> **Jean était à peine sorti quand elle est arrivée.**

> Jean had barely left when she arrived.

Now here are some examples of *ne...guère* :

> **Je n'aime guère ce restaurant.**

> I don't like this restaurant much.

> **On ne voir plus guère ce modèle.**

One hardly sees that model anymore.

Ce n'est guère difficile.

It's not very difficult.

Il n'a guère mangé.

He hardly ate.

Nous ne sommes guère invités chez eux.

We are hardly ever invited to their house.

Je n'y ai guère prêté attention.

I scarcely paid any attention to it.

In most cases *à peine* and *ne...guère* could be used interchangeably, for example *Vous n'avez guère mangé / Vous avez à peine mangé.*

However, in a few cases it would be awkward to use the other expression or they would have different meanings. For example, *Il arrive à peine* means "He's just arrived", but *Il n'arrive guère à parler* would mean "He can hardly talk".

sauf ça
hormis ça
à part ça
à l'exception de ça

The word <u>except</u> is certainly a key word in everyday

conversation. Here are a number of ways to say it in French:

> *J'ai un peu mal au dos. <u>À part ça</u>, tout va bien.*

> I have a little back ache. except for that, everything is fine.

> *<u>Hormis</u> le froid, c'est une belle journée.*

> Except for the cold, it's a beautiful day.

> *Je les prendrai tous, <u>à l'exception de</u> celui-là.*

> I'll take them all, except that one.

> *Elle n'a rien à elle, <u>sauf</u> ses économies.*

> She has nothing belonging to her except / besides her savings.

> *Le magasin est ouvert tous les jours, <u>sauf</u> le dimanche.*

> The store is open every day except Sundays.

malgré
en dépit de

Malgré and *en dépit* de are two ways to say another common expression, <u>in spite of</u>.

Of the two expressions, *malgré* is probably used

more commonly than *en dépit de*. Both of them can be translated as <u>in spite of</u> or <u>despite</u> or <u>notwithstanding</u> *(nonobstant)*.

Malgré la difficulté il a continué.

Il a continué en dépit de la difficulté.

> In spite of / notwithstanding the difficulty he continued.

Il a fait ça en dépit de bon sens.

> He did that contrary to commnon sense.

> He did that even though it didn't make good sense.

Elle a fait ça malgré sa mère.

Elle a fait ça malgré la réticence / les conseils de sa mère.

Elle a fait ça en dépit de la réticence / des conseils de sa mère.

> She did that in spite of her mother's opposition / advice. (Note that *en dépit* requires a <u>de</u> while *malgré* does not)

Malgré la neige on peut encore conduire.

En dépit de la neige on peut encore conduire.

> Despite the snow we can still go by car.

J'ai fait ça malgré moi.

> I did that against my will / inspite of my-self.

à moins que
à moins de

The expresssions *à moins que* and *à moins de* mean <u>unless</u>.

À moins que is followed by a <u>ne</u> and the <u>subjunctive</u> of the following <u>verb</u>.

À moins de, on the other hand, is followed by <u>a noun</u> or <u>an expression</u> rather than a verb.

Thay's probably hard to follow so here are some examples which will make it clear. *À moins que* is used more frequently and we'll look at *à moins que* first:

> *À moins que je ne me trompe, il est arrivé à dix-sept heures.*

> > Unless I am mistaken, he arrived at five in the afternoon.

> *Je préfère ne pas le faire, à moins que vous n'insistiez.*

> > I prefer not to do it, unless you insist.

> *Il va échouer à moins qu'il ne fasse beau-coup plus d'effort.*

He's going to fail unless he makes a lot more effort.

Let's go on now to *à moins de*. Remember that *à moins de* is usually followed by a noun.

> **Nous arriverons à dix-huit heures à moins d'un imprévu.**
>
> We will arrive at six in the afternoon unless something unforeseen happens / barring something unforeseen.
>
> **Il va échouer à moins d'un miracle.**
>
> He's going to fail, barring a miracle / unless there's a miracle.

As with most of the terms I've given you, I've chosen these last three (except, in spite of, unless), because they are extremely useful and, above all, versatile. You can employ them in a wide variety of settings and circumstances. They are expressions that you'll probably need to use almost every day.

nickel

Nickel does refer to the metal nickel. However, in French, **nickel** is also a slangy adjective meaning perfectly clean and proper, impeccable. It's a fairly common expression.

> **J'ai lavé la voiture. --- J'ai vu. C'est nickel !**

I washed the car. --- I saw. It's perfect! / It looks great!

C'est drôlement nickel chez Colette.

Colette's house is <u>really</u> clean!

By extension, *nickel* can be used for anything which is perfectly done and about which there is nothing to criticize.

Ce maçon fait toujours un travail nickel.

That macon always does a perfect job.

It can really be used for anything which you are completely happy about.

Comment ça s'est passé pour l'examen ? --- Nickel !

How did the exam go? --- Perfect!

Side Note: Remember that *nickel* is pronounced with the French *"i"* sound, not the English. It sounds something like "nee-kell".

à la fois

The expression **à la fois** means <u>at the same time</u> or <u>both</u> and is used just like the English expression. For example:

Elle peut être, à la fois, gentille et méchante.

She can be both charming and nasty /
She can be charming and nasty at the
same time.

C'est, à la fois, beau et bon marché.

It's both beautiful and inexpensive / It's
beautiful and inexpensive at the same
time.

Le verbe anglais, to patronize, **peut signifier traiter quelqu'un avec bienveillance apparente mais, à la fois, avec condescendance.**

The English verb "to patronize" can mean
to treat someone with apparent kindness
but, at the same time, with condescension.

avoir lieu

Avoir lieu means to take place. It's pretty straightforward:

Le concert va avoir lieu demain.

The concert will take place tomorrow.

Il va avoir lieu dans la grande salle.

It will take place in the large hall.

L'exposition a lieu cet après-midi.

The exhibition is taking place this afternoon.

La réunion a eu lieu hier.

The meeting took place yesterday.

J'ai bien mangé

In English we would put an adverb like "well" after the main verb and say "I have eaten <u>well</u>". In French the adverb comes after the auxillary verb and before the main verb, as in *j'ai <u>bien</u> mangé*.

If you were to hear a foreigner saying "I have well eaten" you'd understand what they were saying, but you'd think that they didn't speak very good English.

In the same way, if you use the English construction and say "j'ai mangé bien", French people will understand you, but it will sound just as wrong to them as "I have well eaten" sounds to you.

To reiterate, in French, the adverb (such as *bien* or *beaucoup*) usually comes after the auxillary verb and before the main verb, as in:

On a <u>bien</u> mangé

We've eaten well. (You do NOT say "On a mangé bien").

Nous avons <u>beaucoup</u> mangé.

We've eaten a lot.

Ils n'ont _rien_ bu ce soir.

They drank nothing this evening.

J'ai _trop_ bu.

I drank too much.

J'ai _mal_ dormi.

I slept poorly.

Il est _subitement_ parti.

He left suddenly.

J'ai _vraiment_ vu trois bateaux.

I really saw three boats.

J'ai _jamais_ mangé autant de raisins / Je n'ai _jamais_ mangé autant de raisins.

I have never eaten so many grapes. (NOT: _Je n'ai mangé jamais tant de raisins_).

This holds as well when you use other auxillary verbs like _pouvoir, vouloir_ and _aller_. The adverb still comes after the auxillary verb and before the main verb:

Nous allons _bien_ manger chez Jean.

We will eat well at Jean's house.

Note that _Alors, nous allons bien manger chez_

Jean ? could also mean "Then we're really going to eat at Jean's house?" as you will remember from the discussion of *bien* as a word used to intensify.

On peut <u>bien</u> entendre.

One can hear well.

Ils vont <u>bientôt</u> arriver.

They will arrive soon.

Cela veut <u>aussi</u> dire...

That also means...

However, when there is no auxillary verb, as in the present, imparfait, future or conditional tenses, the adverb goes after the verb as in English:

Elle mange <u>beaucoup</u>.

Il mangeait <u>peu</u> quand il était jeune.

Il boit <u>trop</u>.

Elle parle <u>peu</u>.

On mange <u>bien</u> dans ce restaurant.

Nous mangerons <u>bien</u>.

Elle ne dira <u>rien</u>.

Il parle français et il parle <u>aussi</u> italien

Note, however, that when *beaucoup, trop,* and *peu*

don't modify the verb but modifie some object instead, they usually come after the main verb, instead of between the auxillary and the main verb.

This sounded very complicated when I stated it in words but it is very simple when I illustrate it with a couple of examples:

> *J'ai <u>trop</u> bu.* - BUT - *J'ai bu <u>trop de vin</u>.*

> *Elle a <u>peu</u> mangé.* - BUT - *Elle a mangé <u>peu de carottes.</u>*

comme tout

This very nice little expression emphasizes an adjective. **Comme tout** is always positive and can be translated as: <u>very</u>, <u>really</u>, <u>extremely</u>, <u>incredibly</u> or <u>as anything</u>. This is casual rather than formal French, of course.

> **Elle est gentille comme tout !**

> She's really nice.

> **C'est joli comme tout.**

> It's very pretty.

> **Leur chaton est mignon comme tout.**

> Their kitten is as cute as anything.

> **C'était facile comme tout.**

> It was incredibly easy!

Side Note: Don't confuse this expression with *tout comme* which we addressed earlier in the book and which means "just like".

comme ci, comme ça

While we are on *comme*, the little expression **comme ci, comme ça** means <u>so-so</u>, <u>neither good nor bad</u>. It's easy to remember and easy to use.

> **Comment vas-tu ? --- Comme ci, comme ça.**

> How are you? --- So-so.

comme (meaning: in the way of)

The word **comme** can also mean <u>in the way of</u>. What I mean by "in the way of" is also difficult to explain in words, but it is easily illustrated with a couple of examples:

> **Qu'est-ce que vous avez aujourd'hui comme fruit ?**

> What do you have today in the way of fruit.

> **Que veux-tu comme boisson / dessert ?**

> What would you like in the way of a drink / dessert.

> **Comme bagage, il n'avait qu'un sac à dos.**

In the way of baggage, he had only a backpack.

n'avoir rien à voir avec

The useful expression ***n'avoir rien à voir avec*** means <u>to have nothing to do with</u> (someone or something). It says that the two things referred to have nothing to do with each other. For example:

> ***Le mot français, une caution, n'a rien à voir avec le mot anglais,*** caution.

> The French noun, *une caution*, has nothing to do with the English word caution.

> ***Cela n'a rien à voir avec lui.***

> That has nothing to do with him.

> ***Ça n'a rien à voir avec cette proposition.***

> That has nothing to do with this proposal.

Side Note: Be aware that this term is different from *n'y être pour rien (je n'y suis pour rien)*, which we dealt with earlier in the book.

- Although *n'y être pour rien* can also be translated "to have nothing to do with it", that expression is a <u>denial of responsibility</u>:

> ***Je n'y suis pour rien / Elle n'y est pour rien.***

I had nothing to do with it / She had nothing to do with it.

- On the other hand *n'avoir rien à voir avec* simply means that the two things are <u>not related</u>. It has nothing to do with responsibility:

Ça n'a rien à voir avec cette proposition.

That has nothing to do with this proposition.

Pas de problème !
Pas de souci !

The expression **Pas de problème** means <u>No problem</u>!, just as you might expect. You use it as you would use "No problem!" in English. For example: "We'll be about fifteen minutes late. - No problem! We'll be expecting you."

Je crains que nous ne soyons quinze minutes en retard. --- Pas de problème. Nous vous attendrons.

Je n'ai pas de monnaie. --- Pas de problème. Tu paieras demain.

I don't have the change. - No problem. You can pay tomorrow.

Pas de problème is, of course, an abbreviation of *Il n'y a pas de problème*. As an abbreviation it is thus from the *langage familier*. It is widely used.

Another common expression is **Pas de souci !** which has a similar, but not exactly identical, meaning. We discussed *Pas de souci !* earlier as an abbreviation of *Ne te fait pas de souci.*

Specifically, you could translate *Pas de souci !* as No worry! or Don't worry yourself about it!. Most of the time you could use *Pas de problème* or *Pas de souci* interchangeably. For example, in the illustration just above, you could say:

...Pas de souci. Tu paieras demain.

In both languages, *Pas de problème !* and "No problem!" can also simply mean *D'accord !* or "Okay!". Note the the three examples just below. In each of these *Pas de problème !* would be translated by "No problem" or "Okay".

> **Puis-je entrer maintenant ? --- Pas de problème.**

> **Est-ce que tu peux venir demain ? --- Pas de problème.**

> **Puis-je manger une pomme ? --- Pas de problème.**

There is a nuance of difference between *Pas de problème* and *Pas de souci. Pas de souci !* which means "don't worry" just wouldn't be as appropriate a respnse when someone is asking if they can eat an apple.

On the other hand, note the example below, in which

Pas de souci is used to tell someone specifically not to worry about a set of circumstances.

> **Nous voudrions bien vous inviter à rester manger avec nous, mais nous avions prévu de manger les restes et je crains qu'il n'y ait pas assez. --- Pas de souci. On se contentera de ce qu'il y a.**

> We would like very much to invite you to stay and eat with us, but we had planned to eat left-overs and I'm afraid that there won't be enough. --- Don't worry yourself about it. We'll be content with whatever there is.

You could respond:

> **Pas de problème. On se contentera de ce qu'il y a.**

> No problem. We'll be content with whatever there is.

and no one would think twice about your choice of expressions, but *Pas de souci !* is a better choice here, as you are really telling someone not to worry.

d'ailleurs
en outre
de plus

All three of these expressions can be translated as
<u>besides</u> or <u>besides which</u>.

The word "besides" has two different senses in English. The first meaning of besides in English is <u>in ad-
dition</u>. This sense of besides is usually translated by
en outre or *de plus*:

> *Je voudrais quelques pommes, et en outre*
> */ et de plus, je voudrais quelques poires.*
>
>> I'd like some apples. And besides them,
>> I'd like some pears.
>
>> I'd like some apples, besides which I'd
>> like some pears.

The second meaning of besides in English, is <u>more-
over</u>, as if the speaker has had an additional thought
addressing another aspect of the subject. It is this
sense of besides which is usually translated as
d'ailleurs. For example:

> *C'était une vraie bêtise! D'ailleurs, si tu*
> *étais resté chez nous comme je t'ai dit,*
> *ceci ne serait jamais arrivé.*
>
>> It was a stupid thing to do. And besides,
>> if you had stayed home as had told you,
>> this wouldn't have ever happened.

Je ne l'ai pas vue, et d'ailleurs, c'était de sa faute.

I didn't see her. And besides, it was her fault. (After an accident).

Side Note: Since *ailleurs*, by itself, means "elsewhere" in a physical sense, it's difficult to see how the meaning of *d'ailleurs* came from that of *ailleurs*. It undoubtably did at one time, but the meanings have grown apart.

Second Side Note: Note that the English word beside (without an "s") is a different word than besides. Beside means "alongside of" and is not used in the same way as besides.

piger

Piger is a very slangy verb which is the equivalent of to get it or to understand it in English. You wouldn't use it in any kind of formal situation, but it is commonly used in speech among young people.

Tu piges ? or Est-ce que tu piges ?

Do you get it?

J'ai beau expliquer, il ne pige rien.

Even though I expained, he didn't get any of it.

J'ai pas pigé ce qu'il a dit.

I didn't get what he said.

The *ne* is dropped from *je n'ai pas pigé*. Since *piger* is slangy in itself, if you are using it in conversation the context would probably be very informal.

de fil en aiguille

From a very slangy expression we move to a more classical one. ***De fil en aiguille*** literally means "from thread to needle" and implies that one thing happened after another by a natural progression. It can be translated as <u>one thing leading to another</u> or <u>little by little</u> or <u>gradually</u>.

> ***J'ai vu les cerisiers en fleur, et de fil en aiguille, j'ai songé à Claire.***
>
>> I saw the cherry trees in flower and , one thing leading to another, I thought of Claire
>>
>> ...and, little by little, I thought of Claire
>
> ***De fil en aiguille, il m'en a dit d'avantage.***
>
>> Little by little, he told me more about it / He gradually told me more about it.
>
> ***De fil en aiguille, nous avons commencé à parler de Paris.***
>
>> One thing leading to another, we started to talk about Paris.

au fil du temps

This expression uses a different meaning of the word *le fil*. In this case it means "the flow", instead of "the thread". Thus *au fil du temps* means <u>as time flows by</u> or <u>with the flow of time</u> or <u>over the course of time</u>. It doesn't really mean the same thing at all as *de fil en aiguille*. Variations are *au fil des heures, au fil des jours* (as the hours go by, as the days go by).

> **Au fil des jours il a beaucoup amelioré sa déxtérité.**

> > Over the course of several days he greatly improved his skill / his dexterity.

> > As the days went by, he greatly improved his skill / his dexterity.

> **La santé de Pierre s'améliore au fil des jours.**

> > Pierres's health improves as the days go by.

There are other expressions using *le fil* in the sense of "the flow". For example:

> **le fil des événements**

> > the course of events

> **suivre (ou) perdre le fil de la conversation**

> > to follow (or) to lose the <u>flow</u> of the conversation

It's interesting that in English you can use "thread" figuratively and translate this expression as:

> to follow (or) to lose the <u>thread</u> of the conversation

entre-temps

Entre-temps simply means <u>meanwhile</u> or <u>in the meantime</u>. You'd use it whenever you'd use one of these in English.

> **Entre-temps j'avais réussi à finir le travail.**
>
> Meanwhile I had finished the work / the job.

> **Entre-temps il m'est arrivé de rencontrer M. Boucher au Café de la Poste.**
>
> In the meantime I happened to meet Mr. Boucher at the Café de la Poste.

tenir le coup

The expression **tenir le coup** means <u>to hold up under an emotional blow, stress, difficult circumstances, or verbal attack</u>. *Tenir le coup* is proper French and you can use it anywhere.

> **Je lui ai annoncé que son frère était mort et il a bien réussi à tenir le coup.**

I explained to him that his brother is dead and he held up well.

J'ai travaillais dans un grand magasin mais je ne tenais pas le coup.

I worked in a big department store but I couldn't take the stress / but I couldn't hold up.

Il tenait le coup parce qu'il se concentrait sur ce qu'il avait à faire dans les cinq minutes.

He held up / He was able to deal with the stress because he kept concentraiting on just what he had to do in the next five minutes.

à souhait

The expression ***à souhait*** (pronounced "soo-ay"), acts as an adverb and means <u>as much as one could want</u> or <u>as well as one could desire</u>.

On a mangé à souhait.

We ate as much as we wanted / as much as we could eat.

Tout s'est passé à souhait.

Everything went as well as we could desire.

bref

We can handle **bref** very quickly as it is actually in-tuitive in English. *Bref* means <u>briefly</u>, <u>in short</u> or <u>in brief</u> or <u>to sum up in a few words</u>. It's a synonym of *enfin*, is proper French, and can be used anywhere.

> **Bref, ça ne sert à rien.**
>
> In short, that serves no purpose.

avoir la flemme de faire quelque chose

Avoir la flemme *de faire quelque chose* means <u>to be too lazy</u> to do it or <u>to not want to bother</u> to do it or <u>to feel it's too much trouble</u> to do it.

> **Si vous passez à la boulangerie, est-ce que vous pouvez achetez du pain pour moi ? J'ai la flemme d'aller en ville aujourd'hui.**
>
> If you pass a bakery, could you buy a bread for me, I don't have the energy to go into town today.
>
> **Nous avons beaucoup travaillé ces derniers jours. J'ai la flemme de tailler les oliviers aujourd'hui.**
>
> We've worked a lot the past few days. I'm not up to trimming the olive trees today.

jadis
naguère
d'antan
autrefois

Jadis (the "s" is pronounced) and *naguère* are a couple of words that are a bit literary but are very nice to use. They give you ways to speak about the past.

Jadis is used for the distant past and can be translated as <u>in times past</u>, <u>formerly</u>, or <u>once</u>.

Naguère is used for the recent past and can be translated as <u>not long ago</u> or <u>recently</u>.

> **Jadis ces cabanons en pierre abritaient les bergers par mauvais temps.**

> > In olden times these stone cabins sheltered shepherds in bad weather.

> > Once upon a time these stone cabins sheltered shepherds in bad weather.

> **Pour la fête elles portent les costumes de jadis.**

> > For the festival the women wear the costumes of olden days.

> **Naguère c'était un joli champs ici, et regarde maintenant, quel lotissement laid.**

> > Not long ago it was a pretty field here, and now look! What an ugly housing development.

> *Mes compagnons de naguère sont tous partis ailleurs.*

>> My recent companions have all left for other places

I'll throw in one more similar word, even more poetical than *jadis* and *naguère*. This is **d'antan,** which means of olden days.

> *Mais où sont les neiges d'antan ?*

>> But where are the snows of olden days / of yesteryear? (François Villon)

Finally **autrefois** is the current, ordinary, plain, bread-and-butter word which means formerly, in the past, or once.

> *Autrefois ces cabanons en pierre abritaient les bergers par mauvais temps.*

> *Mes compagnons d'autrefois sont tous partis ailleurs.*

>> I'm afraid that find *autrefois* a colorless word without the charm of the first three, which I prefer to use when appropriate, but perhaps that's just a matter of personal taste.

facultatif

There is a French word *optionnel* which means optional, but it isn't used much. The word that you are likely to hear all the time is **facultatif**. Since *facultatif* is frequently used, and not at all an intuitive word for an anglophone, I thought I should include it.

> **Les classes de l'après-midi sont facultatives.**

> The afternoon classes are optional.

> **Un pourboire est facultatif ici.**

> A tip is optional here.

traiter en
traiter de

Traiter en and *traiter de* are expressions that you will hear frequently.

Traiter quelqu'un <u>en</u> means <u>to treat someone as</u> or <u>to treat someone as if</u>.

> **Il m'a traité en intrus.**

> > He treated me <u>as</u> an intruder / He treated me <u>as if I was</u> an intruder.

> **Elle l'a traité en fils.**

> She treated him as if he were her son.

On the other hand **traiter quelqu'un <u>de</u>** means <u>to call someone a name</u>.

> **Elle m'a traité d'idiot devant mes amis.**

She called me an idiot in front of my friends,

Il l'a traitée de tous les noms.

He called her every name in the book.

Note that *elle l'a traité <u>en</u> idiot* means she **treated him as** an idiot, while *elle l'a traité <u>d</u>'idiot* means she **called him** an idiot.

Note also that *traiter* can also be used without the *en* or the *de :*

Il m'a très mal traité.

He treated me very badly.

Elle a très mal traité sa fille.

She treated her daughter very badly.

Il l'a traitée comme une chienne.

He treated her like a dog.

tiré par les cheveux

Tiré par les cheveux means <u>far-fetched</u> or <u>unlikely</u>. It's a rather picturesque expression, literally translating as "pulled by the hairs".

Cette théorie est un peu tirée pas les cheveux.

That theory is a bit far-fetched / is a bit of a stretch.

bel et bien

The expression **bel et bien** acts as an adverb and means that something happened, or was true, <u>after all</u> when it had been uncertain or in doubt.

Il a bel et bien tenu sa promesse.

He kept his promise after all.

Ils sont bel et bien arrivés à l'heure.

They arrived on time after all.

La magnifique théière était bel et bien en porcelaine.

The magnificent teapot was indeed in porcelain.

après coup

Après coup means <u>after the fact</u>, <u>afterwards</u>, <u>looking back</u>, <u>after the event</u>.

Après coup, j'ai pensé à toutes les bonnes réponses que j'aurais pu donner à ses remarques.

Afterwards, I thought of all the good responses that I could have given to his remarks.

cela ne tient pas debout

Cela ne tient pas debout means that <u>it doesn't stand up to examination</u>, <u>it doesn't hold water</u>.

Cette histoire ne tient pas debout.

That story doesn't hold water / That story doesn't make sense.

en vouloir

The expression **en vouloir à quelqu'un** can be translated as <u>to hold something against someone</u> or <u>to hold a grudge against someone</u> or <u>to be angry at someone</u>. It's a common verb form and it's proper French. You can use it anywhere.

Il m'en veut à cause de...

He holds a grudge against me because of...

Ne m'en veux pas.

Don't be angry at me because of it.

Don't hold it against me.

Il en veut à sa soeur de ce qu'elle à dit.

He's still angry at his sister because of what she said.

Side Note: This expression, *en vouloir,* is very easy to misunderstand in speech. Similarly you can skip right past it without catching it while you are reading, because *en vouloir* looks and sounds like it has to do with wishing or wanting something instead of being angry about something. You need to be alert for it as it is a common expression.

à l'improviste

The expression **à l'improviste** is related to the English verb improvise and means <u>on the spur of the moment</u>, or <u>without advance planning</u>.

> **Désolé d'arriver à l'improviste.**
>
>> Sorry to drop by without warning. (*Désolé* is of course short for *Je suis désolé*, but it's how people talk casually).
>
> **Pouvez-vous rester manger avec nous. Ce sera un repas à l'improviste.**
>
>> Can you stay and eat with us. We'll throw together an improvised meal.
>
>> Can you stay and eat with us. It will be a spur of the moment meal.
>
> **Nous avons décidé d'y aller, à l'improviste.**
>
> **Nous avons, à l'improviste, décidé d'y aller.**
>
>> We decided on the spur of the moment to go there.

Jean est passé chez nous à l'improviste.

> Jean came by our house on the spur of the moment.

pas mal

The expression ***pas mal*** has two different uses.

The first meaning of *pas mal* can refer to an amount and mean <u>quite a bit</u>.

> ***Tailler tous les arbres m'a pris pas mal de temps.***
>
> > To trim all the trees took me quite a bit of time.
>
> ***Elle a pas mal de bijoux.***
>
> > She has quite a lot of jewelry.

The second meaning for *pas mal* is as an appreciation, similar to <u>Not bad</u>!

> ***Qu'est-ce que tu penses de ce restaurant ? --- Pas mal !***
>
> > What do you think of this restaurant? --- Not bad!
>
> ***C'est pas mal de tout.***
>
> > That's not bad at all.

laisse tomber !

The expression *laisser tomber* translates word for word as "to let fall" or "to allow to fall". In practice, *laisser tomber quelque chose* means <u>to drop it</u>. It can be used in a literal sense:

> **Quand il l'a vue entrer la pièce, surpris, il a laissé tomber son livre.**
>
> When he saw her enter the room he dropped his book in surprise.
>
> When he saw her enter the room he let the book fall in surprise.

The usage that I want to describe to you though is the figurative. When someone says **laisse tomber !** referring to a **subject of conversation** he is saying <u>Drop it</u>! just as one would say in English. It means that he or she doesn't want to discuss it any longer. Similarly if the person is referring to an **activity** it also means "Drop it, let it go for now".

> **Maman, si je suis très sage aujourd'hui, puis-je aller au cinéma demain ? --- J'ai déjà dit non trois fois. Laisse tomber !**
>
> Mommy, if I am very good today, can I go to the movies tomorrow? --- I've already said "No!" three times. Drop the subject!
>
> **Je vais finir de tailler cet olivier. --- Oh, laisse tomber. On le fera demain.**
>
> I'm going to finish trimming this olive tree.

--- Oh, let it go for now, we'll do it tomorrow.

Ah bon ?

Ah bon ? is a little expression which is very common
in conversation and is full of implications.

Ah bon? means <u>Really</u>?, <u>Is that so</u>?, <u>You don't say</u>!,
<u>I didn't know that</u>! It's said with a definite question in
the voice, and there may also be surprise, and even
puzzlement. You may occasionally even hear a bit
of skepticism.

That's a lot of meanings packed into a little expression, so here are a few examples to show you what
I mean:

> *Je lui ai rendu visite hier. --- Ah bon?*
>
> I visited her yesterday. --- Is that so? Why
> was that?

> *Dans sa jeunesse il a passé cinq années
> en Chine et il parle bien le chinois. --- Ah
> bon ?*
>
> When he was young he spent five years
> in China and he speaks Chinese well. ---
> Really? I didn't know that!

> *Tout à l'heure je pensais aller voir Pierre.
> --- Il n'est pas là. Il est en vacance en
> Bretagne. --- Ah bon ? Mais comment ça
> se fait. Je ne le savais pas, moi.*

In a little while I was thinking of going to see Pierre. --- He's not at home. He's on vacation in Bretagne. --- Really! / Is that so! How did that come about? I didn't know anything about it.

Hier je suis allée aux Galeries Lafayette. --- Ah bon ? Et qu'est-ce que tu as acheté ?

Yesterday I went to Galeries Lafayette. --- Oh really? And what did you buy?

Salut !
Coucou !

Salut ! is a casual greeting. You'd usually use *Salut !* with friends or close acquaintances. It's sort of like Hi! or Hi there!

While *Salut !* is usually used with people you know, it can also be used with people you don't know, as a friendly casual greeting. For example, when you are biking and you encounter people biking in the other direction, the usual greeting in whizzing past would be a fast *Bonjour !* However, some friendly people say *Salut !*

You can also *Salut !* as a casual parting in situations where you might say See you!, See ya!, See you soon!, or Bye! in English.

The *"t"* in *Salut* is not pronounced.

Coucou ! is a playful greeting you'd use on encountering someone who didn't expect to see you. For example, on dropping by a friend's house or apartment unannounced you might say:

Coucou ! Nous voilà !

> Hi there! We're here! / Surprise! We're here!

Or if you're a woman and you see a friend in the street and she doesn't see you, you might say:

Coucou ! C'est moi !

> Hi there! It's me!

Like *Salut*, the expression *Coucou* is one that you'd use primarily with friends or close acquaintances. It's used mostly by girls and women. It would be used by boys and men only in a playful situation and only in talking to a girl (woman), a group of girls, or a mixed group of males and females.

For example, I don't think that a man would say *Coucou* to another man, but he might say *Coucou* to a husband and wife who are friends of his on dropping by their house accompanied by his own wife. And a male university student might say *Coucou !* on encountering two or three girls that he's acquainted with at a café.

Coucou can also be used as a noun, although this is less common. For example,

Salut ! Nous sommes passés vous faire un petit coucou.

Hello there! We came by just to say Hi.

Side Note: *Coucou* is pronounced approximately like "Coo-Coo". It comes from the child's game of hide-and-seek where it means something like "peekaboo". This helps explain its use as a surprise greeting on encountering someone who didn't expect to see you.

si ça te chante

This rather poetical expression is from *le langage familier*. If you translate **si ça te chante** word for word it says something like "if that sings to you". What it means in practice is <u>if that pleases you</u>, <u>if that's what you'd like</u>, <u>if that's what you have a fancy to do</u>, <u>if that's what you want to do</u>.

You will usually hear *si ça te chante* in connection with being asked if you want to do something. For example:

Tu peux l'acheter si ça te chante.

You can buy it if you want to / if that's what you'd like to do.

Viens demain si ça te chante.

Come tomorrow if you feel like it / if it interests you.

Si ça te chante can also be used in the *vous* form or be modified to apply to a third person, as:

Venez demain si ça vous chante.

Come tomorrow if you feel like it.

Tu peux venir avec tes amis, si ça vous chante.

You can bring your friends with you if you would all like to come.

Pourquoi est-elle si subitement partie? --- Rien n'interdit à une femme de prendre un peu de vacances si ça lui chante.

Why did she leave so suddenly? --- Nothing forbids a woman to take a little vacation if she gets the urge / if she feels like it.

Il va venir demain, si ça lui chante.

He's going to come tomorrow, if he decides to / if he feels like it.

Le pianiste joue parfois pour ses amis, mais seulement si ça lui chante / mais seulement quand ça lui chante.

The pianist sometimes plays for his friends, but only if he's in the mood / but only when he's in the mood.

Or the form can occasionally be changed to a question as in:

Est-ce que ça te chante de venir demain ?

Does it interest you to come tomorrow? /
Would you like to come tomorrow?

Si ça te chante and its variations are commonly heard in casual speech.

un truc

Anyone wanting to speak and understand colloquial spoken French <u>must</u> be familiar with this word! _Un truc_ is an <u>extremely</u> common all-purpose word.

You can use **_un truc_** for something you have forgotten the name of, or something you don't know the name of, or something you don't want to bother to name correctly. It's basically a "<u>whatchamacallit</u>" or a "thingumajig", as in:

C'est quoi, ce truc rouge ? / Qu'est-ce que c'est que ce truc rouge ?

What is this red thing?

A-t-elle beaucoup de ces petits trucs ?

Does she have a lot of these little whatchamacallits.

Ils sont chers, ces trucs !

These things are expensive!

Avez-vous besoin de ces petits trucs ?

Do you need these little things? (You either don't know what they are called or you are not bothering to name them).

Un truc can refer to a <u>knack or special skill</u>.

La cuisine, c'est son truc.

Cooking is his thing / his special interest.

Les maths, c'est pas mon truc / son truc.

Mathematics is not my thing / his thing.

Il faut avoir le truc.

You have to have the knack.

Un truc can be a "<u>trick of the trade</u>".

J'ai un truc spécial pour enlever les taches.

I have a special method / product for taking out stains.

Un truc can refer to a <u>special trick to cause an illusion</u>, as in a magic show, or in the theatre, or in oratory, or in trial law, etc. It has an implication almost of cheating. Thus *le trucage* is special effects in cinema, or a fake illusion in another setting, and the verb *truquer* can mean to fake a photograph, to rig an experiment, to rig a soccer match or an election, or, in an accounting sense, to cook the books.

Finally, *un truc* can mean just about anything. It can be undefinable; it's just <u>something</u> or <u>a thing</u>. For example:

Je vais vous dire un truc.

> I'm going to tell you something (It could mean something interesting, something odd, something peculiar, or something important).

Son truc maintenant est le régime.

> Her thing nowadays is dieting. (Note that this use of *truc* doesn't fit the categories above. It's not a special knack, or a trick, or something for which you don't know the name. "Her thing" is one way you'd say it in English. You could also say "Her current passion".)

Je dormais. Je n'ai rien entendu. En ce moment je prends des petits trucs pour m'endormir.

> I was sleeping. I didn't hear anything. Right now I take some little *trucs* to put me to sleep. (It's clear that the little *trucs* are sleeping pills, but this illustrates how people use *truc* casually and throw it in anywhere).

Il lui est arrivé un drôle de truc.

> A really odd thing happened to him.

Mathias le trouvait trop maigre, ce type, pas beau, mais il était droit, il suivait son truc, sa petite conviction.

Mathias found him too thin, this guy, not good-looking, but he was honest, he was following his *truc* (his thing?), he was sticking with his convictions. (Fred Vargas)

Ne répète pas toujours les mêmes trucs !

Don't always repete the same things!

Il admirait la capacité des femmes à aimer les hommes, un truc qui lui semblait sacrément difficile, et pire quand on est moche comme lui.

As for women, he admired their capacity to love men, a thing which to him seemed damned difficult, and worse when one is ugly like him. (paraphrased from Fred Vargas).

I gave so many examples of these different types of uses of *truc* to attempt to illustrate some of the myriad of ways that it's employed in casual speech.

Remember that *truc* is a word from casual verbal language, and while it is not at all vulgar, it's not usually used in written French. However, you might use *un truc* in conversation even in less casual settings, depending on the circumstances.

un truc pareil

This brings us to a nice expression, **un truc pareil**, which means roughly <u>a thing like that</u>. It's usually said in a derogatory tone. Here are some examples.

> *Je n'arrive pas à croire qu'elle ait pu servir un truc pareil.*

> > I cant believe that she could serve something like that.

> *Comment est-ce qu'il peut dire un truc pareil ? / Comment ose-t-il dire un truc pareil ?*

> > How could he say such a thing? / How could he say a thing like that? / How dare he say a thing like that? / How does he dare to say something like that?

If you'd like to make the expression less casual you can change *un truc pareil* to *ça* or *cela*, or to be even more formal, *une chose pareille*.

> *Comment est-ce qu'il peut dire ça / cela ?*

> *Comment est-ce qu'il peut dire une chose pareille ?*

Finally, although it is usually negative, *un truc pareil* can sometimes be said in an admiring tone, as in:

> *C'est formidable ! Je ne croyais pas qu'il puisse réussir un truc pareil.*

It's incredible. I didn't think that he could ever succeed at something like that.

un machin

Un machin is another little word like *un truc,* but it corresponds only with the first use of *truc* I gave you above: something you have forgotten the name of, something you don't know the name of, or something you don't bother to name correctly. That is to say: a "whatchamacallit" or a "thingumajig". If you use it for a person, it means "what's-his-name" (or "her-name").

> *C'est quoi, ce machin rouge ? / Qu'est-ce que c'est que ce machin rouge ?*
>
> What is that red thing?
>
> *C'est un joli petit machin.*
>
> It's a pretty little whatchamacallit.
>
> *Avez-vous parlé avec...avec Machin ?*
>
> Did you speak with... with what's-his-name?

Machin is used less frequently than *truc*, and it would make sense to chose *truc* to incorporate into your active speaking vocabulary, but you should recognize *machin* if you hear it.

Remember that you can't use *machin* for the other

uses of *truc.* It doesn't mean a knack or special skill, a trick of the trade, etc.

Oh-la-la !

Oh-la-la ! is the absolutely French way <u>to register astonishment</u>.

You may be tempted to chuckle and think that no one would actually say something like *Oh-la-la !* in real life, but let me reassure you, even French men don't hesitate to say it when surprised. I've even heard French TV sports announcers say *Oh-la-la !* after a surprisingly good or bad play.

You could think of *Oh-la-la !* as equivalent to Oh! My goodness! or Wow! or Jeez!, but these expressions don't really capture it. You can't really translate *Oh-la-la !*. It's just *Oh-la-la !*

Oh-la-la ! can imply <u>admiration</u> as in:

Oh-la-la ! Quel beau gateau !

Ooh! What a beautiful cake!

Oh-la-la ! can imply <u>concern</u> as in:

Oh-la-la ! Quel problème !

Oh! My goodness! What a problem!

Oh-la-la ! can imply <u>happiness</u> as in:

Oh-la-la ! Quelle chance !

Wow! What good luck!

It can also imply <u>disbelief</u>, as in:

Oh-la-la ! C'est pas possible !

Oh no! It's not possible!

(Remember that *C'est pas possible*, which is spoken French, would be *Ce n'est pas possible* in proper French. I'm telling you how people actually talk in casual conversation. You have to remember to put in the *"ne"* of the *ne....pas* in formal settings or when writing.)

Oh-la-la ! can probably express <u>any other kind of astonishment</u> you can think of, as well.

Finally *Oh-la-la !* can just be used for <u>emphasis</u>, as in:

Oh-la-la ! Je suis épuisé !

Wow, I'm exhausted!

Oh-la-la ! Comme c'est beau !

Oh! How beautiful that is! / Oh! Isn't that beautiful!

Oh-la-la ! Quelle mauvaise caractère !

Oh my goodness! What a bad temper!

You may even hear *Oh-la-la !* extended sometimes to *Oh-la-la, la-la !*

Note that *Oh-la-la !* is just the phonetic transcription of the sound of this exclamation. I've seen it written in one dictionary without the hyphens as *Oh la la !* and in another with accents on the *"a"s* as *Oh là là !* It won't really matter to you. It's something you <u>say</u> and not something that you usually write.

tourner la page

The expression ***tourner la page*** (literally "to turn the page") means <u>to put something behind you and make a fresh start</u>.

> ### *Il faut tourner la page.*
>
> You need to forget about it and make a fresh start.
>
> ### *J'ai décidé de tourner la page.*
>
> I decided to put it behind me and make a fresh start.

une bise
un bisou
un baiser
baiser
embrasser
enlacer

The French words ***bise*** and ***bisou*** are really key words that you <u>need to know</u> and need to be able to understand and use. They are words for a kiss, and kissing is much more common in France than in the United States or in Britain. <u>Much</u>, much, more common!

When you meet someone you already know in the U.S., you usually shake hands. In France, on the other hand, if it's someone you know in a social context, as opposed to a business one, you are almost certain to give them a kiss on the cheek. Even shopkeepers or restaurant proprietors, if you frequent them fairly often and they have become acquainted with you, may offer you a kiss on the cheek when you arrive.

The way you describe this custom is ***faire une bise à quelqu'un*** or ***faire un bisou à quelqu'un*** which both mean to give someone a kiss on the cheek.

<u>I'm going to spend a lot of time on this subject because this is an important social ritual!</u> There are unwritten rules to giving *bises*, which are important to know, and which I am about to describe.

<u>If you are a girl or woman</u> and you enter a room with a group of acquaintances, you exchange *bises* with <u>everyone</u> there, male and female (as long as you already know them), even if there are a dozen people.

<u>If you are a boy or a man</u> you exchange *bises* with all the girls or women, and shake hands with all the men.

If you enter the room and there are some people

that you already know and some you don't, you exchange *bises* with your acquaintances and shake hands with the people you haven't yet met.

Believe it or not, you go through the exact same ritual when you leave the room. If you are a woman, you exchange *bises* with everyone on your way out. If you are a man, you exchange *bises* with the women and shake hands with the men.

As you might imagine, if everyone is leaving at once and everyone is exchanging *bises* with everyone else, it's a lot of fun, but it can become complicated.

It is not unknown to shake the hand of a new acquaintance on entering the room, but at the end of the afternoon or evening, if you have become friendly acquaintances, to exchange *bises* when you part. (In other words, exchanging *bises* doesn't imply that you are intimate friends).

If you are a man and encounter a close male friend or relative who you have not seen for some months or years, you would probably exchange *bises* (and hugs) with him, as a sign of closeness and affection, with no one thinking it unusual. In general, however, as I stated above, men usually shake hands with each other.

Now, how do you go about giving all these *bises*? In giving a *bise* you touch your cheek lightly to the cheek of the other person and lightly brush, or almost brush, the person's cheek with your lips, making a slight kissing sound. Then you switch and do the same on the other side. This would be two *bises*.

You do have to count because people in different regions give different numbers of *bises*, some quitting at two (left cheek, right cheek), some giving three (left, right, left), and some going on to four (left, right, left, right). Thus in Provence, we give three *bises*, but the number may vary in Paris or Bretagne, etc. (I've just learned from one of my friends that it's also three *bises* in Belgium).

The people who give two *bises* tease those giving more, saying they are being excessive, while those who give more *bises* tease those who give fewer about being uptight. When you meet someone from another region there can be a momentary confusion with one person stopping while the other is continuing, but it quickly works itself out.

In general people give a *bise* in placing their hands on the other persons shoulders to steady themselves, rather than giving a full hug.

I mentioned the unwritten rules. Well, another one is that I've observed that many people tend to put their left cheek forward first. If you think about it, there ought to be a rule, because if you put your right cheek forward and I put my left cheek forward, we might bang noses. This one isn't a rigid rule though, and you will encounter some right-cheekers. Just go with the flow.

You will sometimes see people remove their glasses

if the person they are giving a *bise* to is also wearing glasses in order to avoid hooking the glasses.

And in ending a phone call or a letter to a close friend you might say:

Bisous ! or **Grosses bises !**

> Hugs and kisses! (The meaning is the same for both *Bisous* and *Grosses bises*).

or:

Fais une grosse bise à ta femme pour nous / de notre part.

> Give your wife a big kiss for us.

Bise and *bisou* are both from the *langage familier.* They usually mean a kiss on the cheek, such as we have been discussing, but depending on context *un bisou* can also mean a romantic kiss.

The proper French word for a kiss is **un baiser** but it is rarely heard. You'll hear *une bise* or *un bisou* at least twenty times more frequently than *un baiser.* Nowadays while *un baiser* can mean a kiss, it is mostly a more formal word, for kissing a religious object, or for a kiss on the hand or on the forehead, for example. (*Baiser la main à quelqu'un* is interesting because the man is not supposed to actually touch the woman's hand that he is "kissing").

This is complicated by the fact that the <u>verb</u> *baiser* which officially means to give a kiss, in slang has come to mean to screw or to fuck(!) And don't confuse *baiser* with a "z" sound (to kiss or to fuck), with *baisser* with an "s" sound (to lower).

The verb **embrasser** in an older meaning, or in a literary sense, means to embrace or hug, but in current French, *embrasser* has evolved to primarily mean to give a kiss. It is probably the best word to use for giving a kiss on the lips. However depending on context it could also be a kiss given to a child, etc.

> ### *Je l'ai embrassée.*
>
> > I kissed (and hugged) her.
>
> ### *Ils se sont embrassés (sur la bouche). (sur la bouche* is optional for more clarity)
>
> > They embraced and kissed each other.
>
> ### *Embrasse-moi.*
>
> > Give me a kiss (or "Give me a hug" if you are talking to your child).

If you want to talk about just giving someone a hug you should use **enlacer quelqu'un, prendre (ou serrer) quelqu'un dans ses bras, faire un câlin** (which has a sense of giving caresses as well), or **étreindre quelqu'un** (which is more literary language).

Enlacer means to entwine if you are talking about

vines, for instance, and if you are talking about people it means to hug.

Il m'a enlacée et m'a embrassée.

> He hugged me and kissed me / He took me in his arms and kissed me.

Enlace-moi !

> Give me a hug / Take me in your arms / Hold me in your arms.

Prends-moi dans tes bras ! is pretty straightforward. It means "Take me in your arms!" *Prendre quelqu'un dans ses bras* can be used in other forms as well:

Il m'a prise dans ses bras et m'a enlacée.

> He took me in his arms and hugged me.

Note that while **faire un câlin** would mean to give a cuddle and caresses if it was between mother and child, it would mean a hug and caresses between two friends, and, in slang between adults, it can mean making love, depending on context.

Where in English we talk about **giving a hug**, the French talk more about giving a kiss, and thus they don't have a really good **noun** for "a hug". In my English-French dictionaries the only noun translating a hug or an embrace that I could find is the very formal noun, *une étreinte*. The French language simply doesn't make as clear a distinction between a hug and a kiss that we make in English.

To translate the English noun "a hug" into French you could use *un câlin* in casual language or *une étreinte* in more formal language, but neither really captures it.

To translate "Give me a hug" try one of the following:

> *Fais-moi un bisou.* - This is informal. It could be a mother talking to a child.

> *Fais-moi un câlin.* - More affectionate. It could be mother to child or it could be romantic partners. It implies caresses as well as a hug.

> *Serre-moi dans tes bras.* – This is usually romantic but could be used in a non-romantic setting by someone who was feeling sad, for instance, and wanted a friend to give her a hug.

> *Prends-moi dans tes bras !* - This would probably tend to be used fairly exclusively in a romantic context.

> *Viens m'embrasser.* - This can be romantic, implying a kiss as well, but it could be a grandmother talking to her grandchild. It all depends on context.

> *Embrasse-moi !* - This would usually be romantic, even passionate, but the same

caveats I gave in the previous example apply here as well. It depends on the setting and who you are with.

Enlace-moi ! - This is clearly a request for a romantic hug.

Enlace-moi, prends-moi dans tes bras ! - There's no question about what you mean!

To summarize: You are probably best off using *une bise* or *un bisou* for a kiss on the cheek, e*mbrasser quelqu'un* for giving a kiss on the lips with an embrace attached, and *enlacer quelqu'un* for a romantic hug. It's probably best to be very careful in using *un baiser* or the verb *baiser* to avoid any possible confusion.

j'y crois pas

The expression *j'y crois pas* means <u>I can't believe it</u> or <u>I don't believe it</u>, depending on context.

Il a dit qu'il va venir mais j'y crois pas.

He said he will come but I don't believe it.

Franchement, j'y crois pas. C'est pas possible.

To tell the truth I can't believe it! It's not possible!

Side Note: Note that *j'y crois pas* is from the oral language and is not proper written French, which would be *je n'y crois pas.* The same for *C'est pas possible,* which would be *Ce n'est pas possible* in proper French. I'm telling you how people actually talk in casual conversation. You have to remember though to put in the *"ne"* of the *ne....pas* in formal settings or when writing.

Mon oeil !

Mon oeil ! is another wonderfully picturesque way to say <u>I don't believe it!</u> It's roughly equivalent to saying "In a pig's eye!", which is an older expression that you no longer hear very much in English. You do hear *Mon oeil !* though, fairly frequently.

Il dit qu'il l'a fait tout seul. --- Mon oeil !

He says that he did it all by himself. --- No way! I don't believe it.

What adds to the local color is the gesture that some-times accompanies *Mon oeil !* The speaker puts his index finger on his upper cheek (his cheekbone), as if he is pointing at his eye, and pulls down slightly, pulling down his lower lid, at the same time as he says *oeil*. It's very expressive.

Mon cul !
un cul

Cul means backside, buttocks, ass (or arse), fanny,

etc. It's only vulgar to the extent that talking about someone's buttocks or ass would be – that's to say it's impolite, surely, but only mildly vulgar.

Il est tombé sur le cul.

He fell on his backside / ass.

Il est tombé sur les fesses is more polite way of saying the same thing.

Mon cul ! means pretty much the same thing as *Mon oeil !* – that is to say that you don't believe something. It's obviously more vulgar though to say *Mon cul !* than to say *Mon oeïl !*

Il l'a fait tout seul ? Mon cul !

He made that all by himself? My ass! (No way! I don't believe it).

Note that the *"l"* in *cul* is not pronouced so you say *cul* roughly like saying "ku" with a French accent.

un drôle de...

Un drôle de... usually refers to something or somebody <u>funny</u>, <u>strange</u>, <u>odd</u> or <u>peculiar</u>. You'll hear it used frequently, often humorously, and especially in the expression *un drôle de type.*

C'est un drôle de type.

He (or she) is a bizarre character / He's a strange bird / He's a peculiar guy, etc.

You could just as well, however, hear something like:

Nous avons un drôle de chat.

> We have a really bizarre cat (or strange cat). (Usually said affectionately)

Quelle drôle de fille !

> What a strange girl!

Quelle drôle d'idée !

> What an odd idea!

Ça m'a donné un drôle de choc.

> That gave me a helluva shock.

Il lui est arrivé un drôle de truc.

> A really odd thing happened to him.

Et cetera. These examples illustrate how, as with *truc* which we discussed earlier, *un drôle de* is used casually and can be thrown into the conversation in discussing almost any subject.

Side Note: While *un drôle de type* is a bizarre man, *un type drôle* is a funny or amusing guy. It depends on whether the adjective is before or after the noun.

du moins
au moins

The expressions **du moins** and **au moins** both mean <u>at least</u>. At least is a common expression in French as well as in English, and thus you'll hear *au moins* and *du moins* frequently in conversation. They can be used in all the ways that we use "at least" in English as you will see from the following examples:

> **Si au moins elle en avait payé une partie ! / Si au moins il était arrivé à temps !**

> If at least she had payed a part of it! / If at least he had arrived on time.

> **Il était là en juin, du moins il le prétend.**

> He was there in June. At least he claims so / At least that's what he says.

> **Il a au moins soixante ans.**

> He is at least sixty years old.

> **Tu pourrais au moins la laisser parler.**

> You could at least let her speak.

> **C'est du moins ce que je pense.**

> That's at least what I think / At least, that's what I think.

> **Cette femme a été tuée parce qu'elle savait quelque chose, du moins je le crois.**

That woman was killed because she knew something. At least that's what I believe.

Side Note: We discussed *à moins de* and *à moins que* earlier. Both of them mean <u>unless</u>. Don't confuse these expressions with *du moins* and *au moins,* which, as we've just learned, mean <u>at least</u>.

l'addition

If you are thinking about key words that you will need every day, *l'addition* has to rank high on the list. *L'addition* is the bill in any restaurant, café or bar.

L'addition, s'il vous plaît !

Can I have the bill, please.

l'aire

While we are talking about practical everday words, *l'aire* is one that took me a while to figure out when I first traveled in France. When you are driving on the *autoroute* you will see signs frequently for *aires*. It will be *Aire de This 10 km*, or *Aire de That 7 km*, with This and That being place names.

Aires are roadside rests, and before you get to the *aire* there will be signs describing what services are provided at this particular aire, using pictures.

There are two types of *aires*. The first is the type whose signs show just a pine tree and a table. These are just simple rest stops with picnic tables, usually with bathrooms, which, unfortunately, may be substandard.

The second is the type of *aire* whose signs show a gas pump. These *aires* have gas stations with usually a convenience store, snacks, good sandwiches, and reasonably maintained bathrooms.

If the sign has a crossed fork and spoon in addition to the gas pump there may even be one or more restaurants or cafeterias. Thus, this gas station type of *aire* can range from a simple convenience store to a certain degree of elegance. If you are driving in France at all on the *autoroutes*, you will certainly encounter *aires*.

un flic

Here's an everyday practical word that I hope that you won't have too much need for. If you have to deal with the police you are bound to hear the slang expression **un flic**. While it's slang and casual, *un flic* is only mildly pejorative. It's roughly equivalent to <u>a cop</u> in English.

Il faut appeler les flics.

We should call the cops.

Synonyms for *un flic* in more proper French would be *un agent de police* and *un policier*. For the police in general you say *la police*.

Il faut appeler la police.

un gendarme

While we are on the subject of police, **gendarmes** often look and act like policemen but they are actually part of the French military, a special corps in charge of maintaining internal order and public safety. In the countryside, and in small villages especially, they perform the function of policemen. While *gendarmes* may stop you for a traffic infraction, I've also seen them carrying automatic weapons guarding a visiting head of state.

Side Note: As an interesting aside, *gendarmes* are usually not assigned in the region of the country that they come from, and they are rotated around the country every few years, often staying in special barracks. This policy is not accidental but is designed so that the loyalty of the *gendarmes* will be to the nation of France and not to the region of the country in which they are stationed, with the ultimate purpose of preventing any possible separatist movements.

There is another force called the *CRS*, the *Compagnies Républicaines de Sécurité*, which is another internal security force. They are less well known and you are probably unlikely to have any encounter with them.

Mon Dieu !

The exclamation **Mon Dieu !** is a very common way

of expressing astonishment. You will encounter this expression frequently in conversation.

For example, below you have my nineteen year old daughter talking to a shopkeeper. She's reminding the woman, who had not seen her in several years, and who didn't recognize her now that she was a young lady, that the woman's daughter had been her babysitter years before. The shopkeeper's response registers total astonishment.

> ***...Oui, votre fille m'a gardée quand j'étais petite. Je suis la fille de M. Rosenthal. --- Mon Dieu ! Je t'avais même pas reconnue !***

> ...Yes, your daughter was my babysitter when I was little. I'm the daughter of Mr. Rosenthal. --- Oh, my goodness! I hadn't even recognized you! / My God! I hadn't...

As with *Oh-la-la*, which we discussed above, the expression *Mon Dieu* can express all kinds of astonishment. Here below it expresses shock and horror:

> ***Sa fille a été écrasée par une voiture ! --- Mon Dieu ! C'est affreux !***

> Her daughter was run over by a car! --- My God, that's awful!

À bientôt !
À demain !

À bientôt means <u>See you soon</u>. It's a very common expression in casual conversational French. The "soon" can mean you are dashing off and expect to be back in fifteen minutes, or it can also mean that you have just made a lunch date for the day after tomorrow.

À demain is how you say <u>See you tomorrow</u>. It's also used very commonly in conversational French. You'd say it when you part from a friend who you see habitually every day, or someone with whom you have made plans to get together the next day. You can vary *À demain*, to give other meeting dates. For example:

> **À la semaine prochaine.**
>
> See you next week.
>
> **À jeudi, alors.**
>
> See you Thursday, then.
>
> **À mardi prochain.**
>
> See you next Tuesday.
>
> **À plus tard.**
>
> See you later.
>
> **À tout à l'heure.**

See you in a little while.

If you have just made arrangements by phone with a friend to play tennis with him on Sunday, the day after tomorrow, you could hang up saying either *À bientôt* or *À dimanche*.

As you have probably figured out by now, it's the *À* which makes the difference and gives the meaning of a future meeting.

À bientôt, À demain and these other expressions are almost always free standing exclamations and are not meant to be stuck in the middle of a sentence. I have written them starting with a capital *"À"* to help you remember.

C'est de la folie !
La folie, quoi !
à la folie

In a medical sense *la folie* is madness, insanity. But the very common conversational phrase, **C'est de la folie,** refers more to what we would call <u>folly</u> in English. That is to say something which is mad in the sense of <u>very foolish</u>.

C'est de la folie !

It's craziness! / It's madness! / It's nuts! / That's ridiculous!

Inviter tout ce monde à la fois, c'est de la folie !

To invite all those people at the same time, it's madness! / it's nuts!

Comment est-ce que tu peux faire tout ça pour mardi ? C'est de la folie !

How can you do all that by Tuesday? It's madness! / It's impossible!

While *C'est de la folie !* is from informal French, it's not vulgar in any way and you can use it in any informal setting (and even, if appropriate, in a more formal setting).

On the other hand, **La folie, quoi !** is much more informal. It's still not vulgar, but it would only be used in informal settings. My daughter (who is nineteen), says it's used a lot by young people in casual conversation.

J'ai quatre rédactions pour mardi. La folie, quoi !

I have four essays due for Tuesday. It's madness! / It's ridiculous, don't you think?

The expression **à la folie** means madly. For example:

Je l'aime à la folie.

I love him (or her) madly.

And figuratively, **une folie** means an extravagance,

something <u>unreasonable</u>, and, in talking about love, <u>a transient, and sometimes wild, passion</u>.

Elle a acheté un petit haut à bretelles à cent cinquante euros. Une folie, quoi !

> She bought a little top with straps for a hundred fifty euros. What an extravagance!

> Note that if she said **La folie, quoi !** instead of **Une folie quoi !** it would be stronger and mean that the speaker thinks that buying a little top for a hundred fifty euros is madness. (see the discussion of *La folie, quoi !* just above)

Ce n'est pas un véritable amour. Ce n'est rien qu'un coup de folie.

> It's not real love. It's just (unreasonable) passion / a wild passion which won't last.

faute de
faute de mieux

The French noun *la faute* has two basic meanings It can mean fault, mistake or error, or it can mean the lack. The expression **faute de** means <u>for lack of</u>.

Faute d'argent, il n'a pu payer.

> For lack of money, he couldn't pay.

Faute de temps, il ne l'a pas fait / elle n'est pas venue.

For lack of time he didn't get it done / she didn't come.

Faute de mieux means for lack of better, for lack of a better alternative, <u>for lack of a better choice</u>.

Il a bu un mauvais vin, faute de mieux.

He drank a poor wine, for lack of better / as there wasn't anything better.

Elle l'a accepté, faute de mieux.

She accepted it, for lack of better / for lack of a better choice.

tout seul

Tout seul means <u>all by oneself</u>, or <u>all alone</u>. It's a common expression in thoughts like:

Est-ce que tu peux le faire tout seul ? / Peux-tu le faire tout seul ?

Can you do that all by yourself?

Il l'a laissée toute seule.

He left her all alone / all by herself.

Il habite tout seul dans cette grande maison.

He lives all alone in that big house

de toute façon

The expression **de toute façon** means <u>in any case</u>. You can use it in French just as you would use in any case in English.

> **J'ai beaucoup de choses à faire demain, mais de toute façon j'arriverai chez vous à huit heures le soir.**
>
> > I have a lot of things to do during the day tomorrow, but in any case I'll be at your house by eight in the evening.
>
> **Je ne sais pas s'il va neiger demain. De toute façon, il faut partir.**
>
> > I don't know if it will snow tomorrow. In any case, we have to leave.

et qui plus est

The expression **et qui plus est** means <u>and what's more</u> and is used in the same way as its English counterpart. For example:

> **Il a menti, et qui plus est, c'est une calomnie affreuse.**
>
> > He lied, and what's more, it's a terrible slander.

Il est stupide, et qui plus est, il a mauvais caractère.

> He's stupid, and what's more, he has a bad character / and what's more, he's foul-tempered.

au fait
aller au fait
en venir au fait
être au fait
mettre quelqu'un au fait

The short expression ***au fait*** means <u>by the way</u>, and you would use it just as you would use by the way in English.

When you use *au fait* to say by the way, it always starts the sentence. And, while you normally don't pronounce the final *"t" in fait,* you <u>do</u> pronounce it in this expression (so that it sounds roughly like "oh fet" in English).

Au fait is part of the oral language. Here are some examples:

> ***Au fait, qu'est-ce qui est arrivé hier chez vous ?***

>> By the way, what was it that happened yesterday at your house / what happened yesterday at your house.

> ***Au fait, pourquoi est-il venu ici ?***

By the way, why did he come here?

Un fait is a fact, thus *au fait* can be used in some other ways. **Aller au fait** means to <u>go right to the point</u> and **en venir au fait** means to <u>come to the point</u>.

> **Il est allé droit au fait.**
>
> He went straight to the point.

> **Enfin, tu en es venu au fait.**
>
> Finally, you've come to the point, / you've gotten to the point / you've gotten to what you wanted to talk about.

Similarly, **être au fait (de)** means <u>to be informed</u> (about) and **mettre quelqu'un au fait** means <u>to inform someone</u>.

> **Elle est au fait.**
>
> She knows about it / She's up to date on it.

> **Je l'ai mise au fait.**
>
> I brought her up to date / I filled her in.

sa vie durant
de son vivant

> I have to admit that I included these little expressions, not because they are everyday expressions, but simply because I found them attractive and elegant. I hope that you like them too.

De son vivant means <u>during his or her lifetime</u> and *sa vie durant* usually means <u>all his life</u>. They are primarily literary expressions, but you might also hear them in speech.

Il a été malade sa vie durant.

He was sickly all his life.

Sa vie durant, même quand elle était petite...elle écoutait la musique avec une attention exceptionnelle.

All her life, even when she was small, she listened to music with an exceptional attention.

De son vivant il n'était pas reconnu comme grand artiste.

During his lifetime he wasn't recognized as a great artist.

Déjà du vivant de mon mari j'ai eu besoin de travailler de temps en temps / Déjà de son vivant...

Even during my husband's lifetime / Even while my husband was alive, I needed to work from time to time / Even during his lifetime.....

Du vivant de mon père on chauffait avec du charbon, mais maintenant....

During the lifetime of my father / When

my father was alive, they heated the house with coal, but now….

or

The French <u>noun</u> *or* refers to the metal gold, but here we are concerned with the <u>conjunction</u> *or*, which has an entirely different meaning (and has nothing to do with the English conjunction "or" either).

Or marks a transition from one idea to another, or it introduces a particular circumstance in the recital of a story. It can be translated as <u>now</u>, <u>but</u>, <u>nevertheless</u>, or <u>well</u>, depending on the situation, but none of these translations is really exact. *Or* is almost untranslatable.

Or is used more often in written French, but it can certainly be heard in speech as well. Here are some examples of its use:

> **Or, le moment qu'il redoutait arriva / est arrivé.**

> Now the moment he was dreading arrived. (This comes pretty close, but you could also translate it as "Then, the moment…").

> **Il ne boit jamais de vin. Or, hier soir il a bu quatre verres.**

> He never drinks wine. Well, yesterday evening, he drank four glasses / But,

yesterday evening... / Nevertheless, yesterday evening...

Or, un soir, son mari rentra tôt et la trouva avec Pierre.

Well, one evening her husband returned early and found her with Pierre / Then, one evening her husband returned...

Or, à un moment imprévu il...

But, at an unexpected moment he... / Well, unexpectedly he...

histoire de (followed by a verb)
rien que pour
uniquement pour
simplement pour

Naturally, *une histoire d'Angleterre* is a history of England. And whenever *histoire de* is in the form *une histoire de* or *l'histoire de* (and is followed by a noun), it means a <u>history</u>.

However, a simple **histoire de** (without an article), and followed by a verb, is an expression in *langage familier* and means <u>just to</u>, or <u>just in order to</u> .

In order for this explanation to make any sense to you I'll have to give some examples.

Elle t'a raconté des bêtises, histoire de dire quelque chose.

She told you things that were nonsense, just to say something.

Ils sont allés au cinéma, histoire de sortir de la maison / histoire de se distraire.

They went to the movies just in order to get out of the house / just for a little distraction.

Je l'ai dit, histoire de rire un peu.

I said it just for a laugh.

This expression, *histoire de,* is one that you may be relatively unlikely to incorporate into the universe of expressions that you use yourself, but you will certainly hear it used by others. Synonyms in standard French include *rien que pour, uniquement pour, simplement pour.*

Elle l'a fait, histoire de me faire plaisir.

Elle l'a fait, rien que pour me faire plasir.

Elle l'a fait uniquement pour me faire plasir.

Elle l'a fait simplement pour me faire plasir.

She did it just in order to please me.

de bouche à oreille

This one is really simple. The expression **de bouche**

à oreille means <u>by word of mouth</u>. You will hear it spoken and you will use it yourself.

> *Comment est-ce que tu as entendu parler de ce restaurant ? --- De bouche à oreille.*

> How did you hear about this restaurant? —- By word of mouth.

> *Cette nouvelle circule de bouche à oreille.*

> That news is spreading by word of mouth..

au petit bonheur

While *bonheur* means either happiness on the one hand and good fortune or good luck on the other, the French expression *au petit bonheur* means <u>at random</u>. (I agree, it makes no sense, but that's the way it is).

Au petit bonheur is considered proper French and you can use it anywhere.

> *Il se promenait dans les ruelles au petit bonheur.*

> He was wandering through the little streets at random.

> *Il aime beaucoup lire. Il a lu des tonnes de livres, au petit bonheur.*

He loves to read. He's read tons of books, almost at random / without any pattern / on all kinds of subjects.

Elle a eu deux filles, à qui on attribue plusieurs pères, presqu'au petit bonheur.

She has had two daughters, to whom people attribute several fathers, almost at random. *(Les vacances de Maigret – Simenon)*

cinq fois moins

Cinq fois moins is a very common way to say <u>a fifth as much</u> in French. (Similarly for other fractions like *quatre fois moins, trois fois moins*, etc.)

Cinq fois moins makes no sense in English, and sounds bizarre, as in English something can only be five times <u>more</u>, not five times less. We would say "a fifth as much" instead.

Note that for the number one-fifth you can also use *un cinquième*.

Avec ce nouveau traitement il y a trois fois moins de complications chirurgicales.

With this new treatment there are only one third as many surgical complications.

Celui-ci est quatre fois moins cher.

This one costs only a quarter as much.

Cette année la récolte a été deux fois moins que normale .

This year the harvest was only half the size of normal.

An alternate way of saying this last one would be to say:

Cette année la recolte n'a été que la moitié de la récolte normale.

tout à fait

The French expression ***tout à fait*** is used very commonly, both in speech and in literature. When used in a sentence it means <u>absolutely</u>, <u>quite</u>, <u>entirely</u>, or <u>exactly</u>.

When used as a stand-alone exclamation though, *tout à fait* is an expression of agreement and means <u>Exactly</u>! or <u>Absolutely</u>!

Let me give you some examples:

Ce n'est pas tout à fait correct.

That's not entirely correct / not absolutely correct / not quite correct / not exactly correct.

Il n'était pas tout à fait deux heures.

It wasn't quite two o'clock.

Elle ne m'a pas cru tout à fait.

She didn't quite believe me / She didn't entirely believe me.

Ainsi tu crois qu'il va arriver cet après-midi ? --- Tout à fait !

Thus you think he'll arrive this afternoon? --- Exactly! / Absolutely!

Mais oui, c'est tout à fait juste.

Yes, that's exactly right / that's absolutely correct.

C'est vrai ? --- Tout à fait !

Is it true? --- Absolutely !

On ne peut pas en être tout à fait certain.

We can't be absolutely certain about it.

tout de suite

While we are on *tout*, the expression *tout de suite* means <u>immediately</u> or <u>right away</u>. It's a very common expression in everyday speech.

Il va arriver tout de suite.

He'll be arriving right away.

Je vais le faire tout de suite.

I'm going to do it immediately.

Quand ? --- Tout de suite !

When? --- Right away!

sinon

The word *sinon*, can be used in either oral or written language. *Sinon* is *"si non"* (which means "if not"), pushed together, and it can have four different meanings.

The first meaning of **sinon** is "if not" in the sense of "as an alternate choice", which you can translate with <u>otherwise</u>:

> ***S'il fait beau demain j'irai à la plage. Sinon je vais travailler sur mes paperasses.***
>
> > If it's nice tomorrow I'm going to go to the beach. If not, I'll work on my paperwork / Otherwise I'll work on my paperwork.
>
> ***Je partirai peut-être pour Paris cet après-midi. Sinon, je serai chez toi pour dîner.***
>
> > I may leave for Paris this afternoon. If not, I'll come to your house for diner.
>
> ***Vous pouvez passer par la route à droite si vous voulez. C'est plus pittoresque mais c'est plus long. Sinon, allez tout droit, c'est plus direct.***
>
> > You can take the road on the right if you wish. It's more scenic but it's longer. If

not, go straight ahead, it's more direct /
Otherwise, go straight ahead, it's more
direct.

The second meaning of *sinon* is "if not" in the sense
of <u>or the consequences will be.</u>

**Arrête de faire ça ! Sinon, pas de bon-
bons.**

Stop that! Otherwise, no candy for you.

**Il faut le faire comme il nous l'a montré.
Sinon nous allons avoir des ennuis.**

We should do it the way he showed us. If
not, we are going to have problems.

The third meaning of *sinon* is "if not" as <u>maybe even</u>.
You need some examples to understand what I
mean by that:

Je passerai demain matin, sinon ce soir.

I'll come by tomorrow morning, if not this
evening / maybe even this evening.

**Ils en ont acheté des centaines, sinon des
milliers.**

They bought hundreds, if not thousands
/ maybe even thousands.

Il est un des meilleurs, sinon <u>le</u> meilleur.

He's one of the best, if not <u>the</u> best /
maybe even <u>the</u> best.

Finally, we have *sinon* meaning <u>except</u> or <u>except maybe</u>:

> **Il n'y a aucun crime là-bas, sinon des petits délits.**
>
> > There isn't any crime there except maybe little misdemeanors.
>
> **Il ne fait rien, sinon boire du vin rouge et courir après les filles.**
>
> > He does nothing, except drink red wine and chase girls.
>
> **Le long du bar, il y avait des hommes qui ne bougeaient pas, sinon de temps en temps pour lever le doigt, geste que le barman comprenait parfaitement.**
>
> > Along the bar there were men who hardly moved, except maybe from time to time to lift a finger, a gesture that the barman understood perfectly. (Simenon)

ça --- (as a pejorative)

The word *ça* is usually just an abbreviation for *cela* (or *ceci).* However when *ça* refers to a person or to a group of persons it is very familiar and often quite pejorative.

You probably shouldn't take a chance using *ça* this way yourself unless you are very sure of your companions and your setting as you risk appearing rude, but you should recognize this expression if you hear it. Here are some examples:

> **Claire a dit que tu étais là. --- Oh ! Ça ment toujours.**
>
> Claire said that you were there. – Oh! That (one) lies all the time.

> **Les gens riches, je n'essaie pas de les comprendre. Ça ne pense pas, ça ne sent pas comme nous.**
>
> Rich people, I don't (even) try to understand them. They don't think, they don't feel, like us. (from *Maigret a peur* by Simenon)

> **Ça raconte des histoires.**
>
> He / She makes up stories.

> **Elle m'a encore raconté un problème avec son mari. --- Ça se plaint toujours.**
>
> She told me again about a problem with her husband. --- That one feels sorry for herself all the time.

> **Les hommes, soupire Lizbeth, il faut toujours que ça fasse les malins.**
>
> Men! sighed Lizbeth, They always have to act clever / to act like they know everything.

Ça arrive en retard et ça veut qu'on l'attende.

> That one arrives late and wants us to wait for him / her.

You can see how clearly pejorative this usage of *ça* usually is, and why I suggested that you use the utmost caution in using it. You should be aware, however, that *ça* is <u>not always</u> pejorative when used like this. For example:

Nous avons les petits enfants à la maison et ça court partout.

> We have the grandchildren at the house and they run around everywhere. (Affectionate in this case).

un point, c'est tout !

Un point, which means the period punctuation mark at the end of a sentence, can be used figuratively for emphasis in the same way as we use <u>Period</u>! in English:

Tu ne peux pas sortir ce soir. Un point, c'est tout !

> You can't go out tonight, period ! (parent to child)

Je vais pas le faire ! Un point, c'est tout !

I'm not going to do it! Period! End of discussion!

This expression is very much a part of the spoken language as opposed to the written language. It tends to be used in informal settings, with plenty of emotion. For this reason, I didn't hesitate to leave off the *ne* in *Je ne vais pas le faire.* The way it would be said in practice, and the way you'd hear it is: *Je vais pas le faire !*

tout court

The French expression *tout court* also can be translated as <u>period</u>. In this sense it means that nothing else was said.

> **Il a répondu tout court que non.**

> > He just answered no, period / He just answered no (and that was all).

Sometimes *tout court* says period with a different nuance. For example:

> **Je n'aime pas les gamins comme lui ! ---**
> **Tu n'aimes pas les gamins, tout court.**

> > I don't like kids like him! --- You don't like kids, period.

As you can see, here *tout court* cut the descriptive adjective off what the previous person had said and generalized it. Here's another example:

Je n'aime pas les examens de maths.
--- Moi, je n'aime pas les examens, tout
court.

I don't like math exams. --- As for me, I
don't like exams, period!

terre à terre

The expression **terre à terre** can be used both in
spoken and written French. It means down-to-earth,
matter-of-fact, mundane or prosaic, and it can apply to a person, a discussion, or an action. Here are
some examples:

Il a un esprit terre à terre.

He is a down-to-earth person.

Ses soucis sont les préoccupations terre
à terre du ménage.

Her worries are (just) the mundane
household preoccupations.

(Maigret talking on the telephone). **Autre**
chose. Combien de draps de lit y a-t-il
dans la maison ? ... Oui, je m'en excuse,
je sais que c'est fort terre à terre, en effet.

Another thing. How many bed sheets
are there in the house ... Yes, I know.
It's a very mundane question. (from Simenon).

tout à coup
tout d'un coup
d'un coup
soudain
soudainement
subitement
brusquement

A lot of the key expressions in French have a *tout* in them. ***Tout à coup*** and ***tout d'un coup*** are two more. These two mean <u>all of a sudden</u> or <u>suddenly</u> and can be used whenever you'd use suddenly in English. *Tout d'un coup* is sometimes abbreviated as just ***d'un coup*** in very casual speech.

> ***... et tout à coup il a dit...***
>
> ...and suddenly he said...
>
> ***Tout à coup elle s'est sentie très mal.***
>
> Suddenly / All of a sudden she felt very sick.
>
> ***Il faisait frais tout le mois de mai, et maintenant, (tout) d'un coup, il fait très chaud.***
>
> The weather was cool all the month of May and now, all of a sudden, it's very hot.
>
> ***L'hiver est arrivé tout d'un coup.***
>
> ***L'hiver est arrivé tout à coup.***

Winter has arrived suddenly.

L'amour, croyait-elle, devait arriver tout d'un coup.

She believed that true love should arrive in a sudden flash. (Flaubert)

Some other ways to say suddenly in French are **soudain**, **soudainement, subitement** and **brusquement**. You'll hear all of them in conversation as well as *tout à coup* and *tout d'un coup*.

Soudain elle s'est sentie très mal.

Subitement elle s'est sentie très mal.

Brusquement elle s'est sentie très mal.

L'hiver est arrivé soudain.

L'hiver est arrivé soudainement.

Il a changé brusquement.

que dalle or que dal

The French slang expression **que dalle** or *que dal* means <u>nothing at all</u>, <u>nada</u>, <u>not a damn thing</u>. *Que dalle* is used in casual conversation and would not be appropriate for formal conversation or for a formal letter. For example:

Ça lui coûterait quoi, d'appeler Jean ? Que dalle !

What would it cost her to call Jean? Not a darn thing! / Nothing at all! / Nada!

Quel était le résultat de la fouille ? --- Que dalle !

What was the result of the search? --- Nothing at all! / Not a damn thing! / Nada!

Il y a trop de brouillard. J'y vois que dalle !

There's too much fog. I can't see a damn thing!

Je ne peux pas le supporter !
C'est impossible à supporter !

In English, to support usually means to bear the weight of or to hold up. However, in a literary and figurative sense, it can sometimes mean to endure or put up with, usually in a sentence like: It's hard for him to support the grief (or the pain, or the heat).

In French, as well, while *supporter* certainly means to support or bear the weight of *(soutenir)*, it often means to <u>endure, tolerate, or put up with</u> *(endurer, souffrir, accepter)*. And it can refer to a person as well as an emotion.

The two expressions we are discussing here, *je ne peux pas le supporter* and *c'est impossible à supporter*, are commonly heard in conversation and you can feel comfortable in using them whenever you'd want to say that you have trouble putting up with something or someone.

Je ne peux pas le supporter.

I can't tolerate him (or it) / I can't put up with him.

J'ai souvent eu besoin attendre plusieurs heures là-bas et je ne peux pas le supporter.

I've often had to wait several hours there and I can't endure it / put up with it.

C'est difficile / impossible à supporter.

It's difficult / impossible to put up with.

In casual conversation the *ne* is often dropped from *ne....pas* and you will frequently hear simply

Je peux pas le supporter.

avoir raison
avoir tort
se tromper

These are important words because they are how you say that someone is right or wrong, or that he is making a mistake.

The expression *avoir raison* means <u>to be right</u>. Here are some examples of it's use:

On dirait que Jean a eu raison d'arriver si tard.

> It seems that Jean was right to come so late.

Mais j'ai raison !

> But I'm right.

Il a eu raison de partir.

> He was right to leave.

Oui, vous avez bien raison.

> Yes, you are absolutely right.

In a similar way, *avoir tort* means <u>to be wrong</u>. It's used the same way.

On dirait que Jean a eu tort d'arriver si tard.

> It seems that Jean was wrong to come so late.

Pierre a eu tort de partir ce soir.

> Pierre was wrong to leave this evening.

Non, tu as tort de faire ça avec un marteau.

> No, you are wrong to do that with a hammer.

The verb **se tromper (de)** is another way to say to be wrong, to make a mistake, or to make an error. You will encounter both *se tromper* and *avoir tort* frequently and you can use either of them. They are both very acceptable whether in speaking or in writing.

Oh, je me trompais !

Oh, I was making a mistake / I was wrong.

Tu te trompes.

You're making a mistake / You've got it wrong.

Tu peux te tromper comme tout le monde.

You can make a mistake like anyone else.

Il s'est trompé de route / de date.

He took the wrong route / He was wrong about the route / He was wrong about the date.

avoir (instead of *être*)

In *avoir raison*, which we have just discussed, the French use *avoir* (to have) *raison* where we would say to be right. French uses *avoir* (to have) in many other everyday expressions that we would construct in English with to be instead of to have.

215

You may still be wondering what in the world I'm talking about, so think of "I am cold". The French say "J'ai froid". Literally that says "I have cold". Here are some more examples:

J'ai froid.

J'ai chaud.

J'ai faim.

J'ai soif.

J'ai peur.

J'ai raison.

J'ai tort.

J'ai vingt ans.

J'ai mal (partout).

I'm cold (I am cold).

I'm hot.

I'm hungry.

I'm thirsty.

I'm afraid.

I'm right.

I'm wrong.

I'm twenty years old.

I hurt / I am hurting (all over).

These are, of course, all very common expressions. They can naturally be modified to fit the person involved, as well as to the past or future. They keep some form of *avoir* though, even though we would use a tense of to be. For example:

Prends ta veste. Tu vas avoir froid.

Take your jacket. You are going to be cold .

Il était content d'avoir enfin chaud.

He was happy finally to be warm.

Qu'est-ce que tu as ?

This brings us to another nice expression using *avoir*. **Qu'est-ce que tu as ?** literally says "What do you have?". However, what it means is What's the matter? What's wrong? What's bothering you? It's usually an expression of concern among close friends and in this case it's spoken with concern.

Tu me sembles très triste. Qu'est-ce que tu as ?

You seem to me to be very sad. What's wrong?

Between close friends, especially among the young, *Qu'est-ce que tu as* can be abbreviated as:

Qu'est-ce que t'as ?

What's wrong? / What's the matter?

Remember that abbreviating *tu as* as *t'as* is definitely not standard French, and should <u>not</u> be used in writing, or even in a more formal conversational setting. *Qu'est-ce que t'as*, however, is how you are likely to hear it said among young people.

tu m'as eu

And one more common expression from the *langage familier* using *avoir*, **tu m'as eu,** literally saying "you had me", means <u>you fooled me</u>, or <u>you got me</u>.

Tu m'as eu is usually said in a playful way, referring to a small pleasantry. However, other forms of this expression can be used for something more serious, which you are actually angry about. For example:

Là, tu m'as eu. or Tu m'as eu sur celui-là. or Tu m'as bien eu cette fois.

You got me on that one. / You fooled me on that one. (These would be in a playful context).

Il t'a eu.

He got you. He fooled you. He took you in. (Playful or serious).

Je suis fâché. Il m'a vraiment eu.

I'm angry. He really fooled me / He really conned me. (Serious).

passer un examen / le bac

Passer un examen can really mislead you. In French, if you say *J'ai passé un examen* it doesn't mean you passed an exam, it means you <u>took an exam.</u>

> **Je me fait beaucoup de soucis. Je vais passer le bac dans deux semaines.**
>
> I'm very worried. I'm going to take the bac in two weeks.
>
> **Il a passé l'examen de maths mardi.**
>
> He took the math exam Tuesday.

clouer le bec à quelqu'un

The expression **clouer le bec à quelqu'un** means <u>to shut the person up</u>, usually by a pertinent remark or even a threat. It is *très familier* and should only be used in very casual settings and never in writing.

> **Ton observation / Ta remarque lui a vraiment cloué le bec.**
>
> Your remark really shut him up.
>
> **Tais-toi, ou je vais te clouer la bec !**
>
> Shut up or I'll shut you up! (Literally, this

says or I'll nail your beak closed. It's very aggressive.)

Tais-toi !
Boucle-la !
Ferme-la ! or *La ferme !*
Ferme ta bouche !
Ferme ta gueule !
Ta gueule !

All of these expressions are ways of saying Shut up!. For example:

Tais-toi ! which is proper French for Shut up! or Keep quiet !

Boucle-la ! which is slang for Shut up! (literally: Buckle it!)

Ferme-la ! and *La ferme !* both of which are slangy short forms of:

Ferme ta bouche ! which means Shut your mouth!, Then, to be more vulgar, we have:

Ferme ta gueule ! which means something like shut your trap, and is, itself, sometimes abbreviated as just:

Ta gueule ! These last two are considered vulgar. They might be said in great anger or in an attempt to intimidate. The actual meaning of *gueule* is the mouth of an animal such as a dog. However it's conceivable that *Ferme ta gueule* could also be used playfully in joking between friends.

None of these expressions are polite, but they are arranged roughly in order of increased vulgarity. *Boucle-la,* for instance is just slangy while *Ferme ta gueule* is both slangy and vulgar.

Here are some examples of their <u>use in context</u>:

Ta gueule ! Tu ne comprends donc pas que c'est grave ?

Be quiet! Don't you understand that it's serious?

Tais-toi ! Rappelle-toi que nous sommes dans un restaurant. Tu es trop bruyant.

Be quiet. Remember that we are in a restaurant. You are being too noisy. (This might be mother to child).

And finally some examples using *fermer, boucler* and *taire* <u>in other forms</u> but with the same sense of keeping quiet:

Prends exemple sur Pierre. Il la ferme, lui.

Use Pierre for an example. He knows how to keep quiet, that one.

Je croyais qu'il fallait la boucler.

I was thinking that we need to keep quiet

/ that it's necessary to keep our mouths shut.

Nous avons promis à Pierre de la boucler.

We promised Pierre not to say anything / We promised Pierre we'd keep quiet (about it).

Elle fait trop de bruit. Il faut la faire taire.

She's making too much noise. We need to get her to be quiet / to keep her quiet. (Said about a child or a dog for instance).

Tu ferais mieux de la boucler (là-dessus).

You'd do better to keep quiet / to keep your mouth shut (on that subject).

Merde !
Merde, alors !
Mince !
Mince, alors !
Zut !
Zut, alors !
Putain !
Putain de... !

Here's our collection of nasty (and mildly nasty) words. In general these words are at least *familier* if not vulgar, and should be used primarily in very casual conversation. I have indicated in the text which of these words are considered outright vulgar.

Merde is a vulgar noun that means shit. You can translate it to yourself either as <u>shit</u> or <u>damn</u>. As with shit in English, *Merde !* and *Merde, alors !* are common ways of expressing disappointment or disillusionment.

> ### Le marché était hier. Nous l'avons raté. --- Merde !
>
> The market was yesterday. we missed it. --- Shit! / Damn!
>
> ### Merde, alors ! Il est vraiment en retard.
>
> Damn! He's really late.
>
> ### Merde, je ne m'attendais pas à ça.
>
> Oh shit! I didn't expect that.

Merde ! is now in common use among the young, and where thirty of forty years ago it would have been considered very vulgar for an adult to say *Merde,* you may now hear it being used by people of all ages.

Back when *merde* was considered <u>really</u> vulgar, **mince** and **zut** were common substitutes to express the same disappointment. Now that *merde* is used all the time, *mince* and *zut* are less used. It's a shame though, as they are fun words to use, especially if you are not confortable going around saying *merde* all the time. I really prefer saying *Mince !* or *Zut, alors !* myself.

Remember that the *"u"* in *zut* is the French *u* and is not pronounced like the u in the English word hut, nor exactly like the u in the English words lute or flute. To my anglophone ear *Zut !* sounds pretty much like Zoot, but with the "oo" a little swallowed.

> **Mince alors ! Je ne m'attendais pas à ça.**

> **Zut alors ! Je ne m'attendais pas à ça.**

> Damn! I didn't expect that.

> **Zut ! Nous avons raté l'avion.**

> Oh, hell! We've missed the plane.

> **Mince ! J'ai perdu mes clés.**

> Darn, I lost my keys.

> **Zut ! J'ai perdu mon sac.**

> Darn! I lost my purse.

> **Ah ! Mince ! Je peux pas les trouver.**

> Oh damn! I can't find them.

Mince (but not *zut),* can also sometimes just express astonishment rather than being an equivalent of Damn!

> **Mince ! Il l'a vraiment fait !**

Wow! He really did it! / Jeez! He really did it!

And while we are on curse words, **Putain !** is another common word, at least as vulgar as *merde*. *Putain* means <u>whore</u> or <u>hooker</u> as a noun, but when used as an exclamation, it's more like <u>Damn!</u> and can express astonishment, disappointment, anger or even admiration(!) (For admiration, think of "Damn! He ran that race fast!").

> **Putain ! Il l'a vraiment fait !** (astonishment)

> **Putain ! Nous avons raté l'avion.** (disappointment)

> **Putain ! T'es con ou quoi ?** (anger)

> **Putain ! Il a couru vite !** (admiration)

> **Putain de... expresses exasperation.**

> **Ce putain de chat a fait beaucoup de dégâts.**

>> That damn cat made a lot of mess / did a lot of damage.

> **Putain de téléphone ! Tu n'arrêtes pas de sonner !**

>> You damn telephone! Don't you ever quit ringing?

> **Quel putain de temps !**

What terrible weather!

It's probably safest not to use *Putain !* yourself, but you should recognize and understand it if you hear it.

Many expressions in France (as in the U.S.), may be heard more frequently in one region than another. *Putain !* is probably heard more in Provence and in the south of France than in the north.

dans la merde
dans le pétrin

Dans la merde roughly means <u>in a hell of a fix</u>, or <u>up shit's creek</u>. It, also, is a fairly common expression.

> *Je suis bien dans la merde.*

>> I'm really in a fix, everything has gone wrong.

> *Il a encore été viré. Maintenant il est vraiment dans la merde.*

>> He's been fired again. Now he's really in a pickle / really up shit's creek.

Another slangy, but not at all vulgar, way to say the same thing is *dans le pétrin*. *Dans le* pétrin is perhaps a little dated now, but it's still used.

> *Il est vraiment dans le pétrin.*

He's really in a fix / He's really up a creek.

If you are in a situation where using any slang simply isn't appropriate, try:

Il a vraiment de gros problèmes.

Il a beaucoup d'ennuis.

He has lots of problems.

dans de beaux draps

Dans de beaux draps is a related expression. It means <u>in a difficult situation</u>. It's ironic or sarcastic as it literally means "in beautiful sheets". Saying "Il est dans de beaux draps" is like "Well, he's in a wonderful situation" sarcastically. My impression is that it's used for more temporary situations than *dans la merde* (which can be semi-permanent). Here are some examples:

C'est un pneu crevé ! Nous voilà dans de beaux draps !

It's a flat tire! <u>Now</u> we're in a fix! / Boy, <u>we're</u> in great shape! (said sarcastically)

Oh ! tu me mets dans de beaux draps !

Oh! You really put me in a difficult situation!

un emmerdeur / une emmerdeuse

And, for one last *merde* word, **un emmerdeur** can have two related meanings:

First, *un emmerdeur* can be <u>someone who is particularly annoying or *embêtant*</u>, a real pain in the ass, *un casse-pieds*, someone who pisses you off.

Or, *un emmerdeur* can be <u>someone who messes things up for other people</u>.

Oh ! C'est une vraie emmerdeuse !

Oh! She's a real pain! / Oh! She's here just to mess things up!

As you might guess, *un emmerdeur* is very *familier*, even mildly vulgar, and you shouldn't use it in more formal situations or in writing.

une crapule

While we are on people like that, **une crapule** is a term you'd use for someone you have disgust for. It means he's <u>a scoundrel of the worst sort</u>, someone very dishonest.

C'est une crapule !

He's awful, dishonest, a crap-head, a crook and a scoundrel.

Side Note: Note that it's <u>une</u> *crapule,* even when you are talking about a man, because *"ule"* is a feminine noun ending. (See my book *The Rules for the Gender of French Nouns* for a further discussion of this and other rules of gender).

con
connerie
conard, connard
conasse, connasse

To finish up with our "cuss words", **con** as an adjective just means <u>stupid or idiotic,</u> but it is listed as *très familier !* As it's very pejorative you can translate it as <u>damn stupid.</u> You'll remember that we used it in an example above as: *Putain ! T'es con ou quoi ?*

As a noun, **un con** is <u>an idiot</u> or <u>an imbecile</u>, and it also is used pejoratively, of course.

More pejoratively still, and more vulgarly, *il est un con* can mean something like <u>*he's a stupid bastard!*</u> I'm sorry that I can't give you exact translations, but since these are epithets they are hard to translate exactly.

Finally, in a separate meaning altogether, *le con* is a vulgar word for the <u>female sex organ</u>, sort of like cunt. (a French synonym is *la chatte).*

Here are some examples of *con* as an <u>adjective</u> meaning stupid:

Putain ! T'es con ou quoi ?

Goddamn! Are you an idiot or what!

Qu'est-ce qu'il peut être con !

Can he ever be stupid!

Elle est vraiment con ! or *vraiment conne !* (Both forms may be used in talking about a female or something feminine).

She's really stupid!

Now some examples of *con* as a <u>noun</u>:

Quel con !

What a bloody imbecile!

C'est une vraie catastrophe, mais toi, tu t'amuses. Tu en profites pour faire le con.

It's a real catastrophe, but you, you make jokes. You take advantage of the situation to act like a damn imbecile.

C'est un vieux con !

He's an old imbecile / a stupid bastard / a damn imbecile from way back!

There are also several other words that derive from *con*. To start with *une connerie* is <u>stupidity</u>, <u>imbecility</u>, or <u>a stupid action</u>.

Quelle connerie !

What stupidity!

Il fait des conneries.

What he's doing is stupid and absurd.

Arrête tes conneries !

Quit doing those stupid things!

Our final derivative words are **un conard**, **une conarde** and **une conasse**. *Un conard* and *une conarde* are basically synonyms for a male *con* and a female *con*, but worse!

Une conasse is a female *con* and only has a female form. *Une conasse* is very vulgar, more like *une salope* or *une pute !*

All three of these epithets can also be spelled with two *"n"s* as in *connard, connarde* and *connasse.*

T'es fou, ou quoi ?

T'es fou, ou quoi ? is a very casual, but not vulgar, expression which means <u>Are you nuts, or what?</u>

C'est trop dangereux. T'es fou, ou quoi ?

That's too dangerous. Are you nuts? / Have you lost your mind?

Remember that abbreviating *tu es* by *t'es* is definitely not standard French, but goes along with the extreme casualness and the urgency of the question. In a less casual situation you'd have to say it a whole different way. For example:

C'est trop dangereux. C'est de la folie !

Or even more formal:

> *C'est trop dangereux. Je ne suis pas d'accord.*

bouffer
la bouffe

Originally, the verb *bouffer* was a slang word which meant to eat large quantities of food which wasn't especially good (as in a military mess for instance). Now *bouffer* is used more generally as a very slangy word for <u>to eat</u> but it usually keeps its negative connotation. *Bouffer* is used only in very casual settings but it is not vulgar.

> *J'ai envie de bouffer.*

> I'm ready to eat.

> *Et si elle a peur ? --- Il faut bouffer. Personne n'a peur de quelqu'un qui bouffe.*

> What if she's afraid? --- We need to be eating. Nobody's afraid of someone who is shoveling in food.

> *On bouffe toujours plutôt mal chez eux.*

> We always eat rather poorly at their house.

And figuratively:

> *Son travail le bouffe complètement.*

His work totally consumes him.

The <u>noun</u>, *la bouffe* refers either to the act of eating or to the food that you are eating:

> ***C'était une bonne bouffe.***
>
> > It was a good meal / a good feed. (Here *bonne* modifies *bouffe* and thus allows it to be positive).

C'est quoi, ça ?
C'est quoi, ce truc ?

> These expressions are heard in informal conversation and mean roughly <u>What in the world is that thing</u>?
>
> > ***Tu l'as vu, ce truc-là ? --- Non. C'est quoi, ça ?***
> >
> > > Have you seen that thing? --- No. What is it? / What in the world is it?
> >
> > ***C'est quoi, ce truc ?***
> >
> > > What is that thing?

Ça crève les yeux !

> The verb *crever* means to burst, split or explode. Therefore, *Ça crève les yeux !* translated word for word means "That explodes the eyes".
>
> Thus, colloquially, ***Ça crève les yeux !*** means <u>it's</u>

<u>so obvious that you can't miss it!</u> You use it to say that something is pretty obvious, that it jumps right out at you.

> *Elle est jolie comme un rêve. Tu t'en es rendu compte, je suppose ? --- Ça crève les yeux !*

> She's as pretty as a dream. You've noticed, I suppose ? --- You can't miss seeing it!

> *Tu le trouves très beau, n'est-ce pas? --- Oui, mais comment tu l'as su ? --- Ça crève les yeux.*

> You find him very handsome / attractive don't you ? --- Yes, but how did you know? --- It's pretty obvious.

du coup

The expression *du coup* is placed in between an event and it's result and means <u>in consequence</u>, or <u>as a result</u>. To help you remember, you can think of *du coup* as literally meaning "from the blow", and thus figuratively "as a result of what happened".

For example:

> *Tu m'as interrompu, et du coup j'ai oublié ce que j'étais en train de dire.*

> You interrupted me and now I can't remember what I was saying.

Mon mari est malade. Du coup il faut an-
nuler pour ce soir.

My husband is sick. As a result, we have
to cancel for this evening.

Santé !
Santé et amitié !
À la vôtre ! or À la tienne !
Chin-chin !

These are <u>toasts</u> that you'd give around a table with
friends.

Santé ! – To health!

Santé et amitié ! – To health and friendship!

À la vôtre ! – To your health! (Usually in a
one-to-one situation). It could be *À la tienne*
in a situation where you'd use *tu*.

Chin-chin ! - There is no translation as far as
I know. You can think of it as something like
"Cheers!".

un goûter
un apéritif
un apéritif dînatoire
une entrée
un plat
le plat principal
le plat du jour

These are a series of food and meal terms and are key words to know.

Un goûter is equivalent to an English afternoon tea. It is served roughly at about four in the afternoon. *Un goûter* usually involves sweets and is a favorite of children. You can think of it as an afternoon snack.

Adults will occasionally have *un goûter*, but not usually. They are much more likely to have **un apéritif**, which normally is served about six to seven in the evening, and is meant to be a lead-in to dinner. *Un apéritif* usually includes drinks with alcohol, and some little snacks on the order of olives or nuts, or maybe other finger foods.

Un apéritif is <u>not</u> at all like a stand-up-and-circulate cocktail party. You can have *un apéritif* with a friend, or several friends, seated at a table outside a café. If you are invited to someone's house for *un apéritif*, if it's nice weather you are likely to be seated with one to two or three other couples around a table on a *terrasse*, with the drinks and nibble-food on the table. If it's cooler weather, you will probably be in the *sa-*

lon, seated around a coffee table *(une table basse),* again with the food and drinks on the table.

Sometimes *l'apéritif* can simply refer to the drink:

> **Qu'est-ce que vous voulez comme apéritif ?**
>
> What would you like for an apéritif?
>
> **Celui-ci est un apéritif provençal.**
>
> This one is an apéritif from Provence.

Occasionally, *un apéritif* (the drink) may be served just before lunch but this is somewhat less common.

Un apéritif dînatoire means that it's not a sit-down dinner but that there will be enough food served with your drinks so that you won't go home hungry. You can think of it as a buffet, but it's not a get-up-and-go-serve-yourself type buffet. You will be seated around a table as I described for an *apéritif,* the food will be in attractive serving plates or bowls arranged on the table and you will serve yourself or pass the food around.

Un apéritif dînatoire might include cold shrimp, little sausages, raw vegetables with a dip, some little toasts with spreads, clearly more than you'd have at an ordinary *apéritif.*

You shouldn't think however that there is a hard and fast distinction between a simple *apéritif* and *un apéritif dînatoire*. There's everything in-between, and often an ordinary apéritif may take the place of dinner if it lasts long enough and everyone is having a good time. You can get pretty full on nuts and olives.

In American English, at least, the entrée has come to mean the main course, inspite of entrée obviously meaning the entrance to the meal. In France, *l'entrée* has kept its natural sense and means the first course or appetizer. When you see *entrées* on the menu, it's referring to the appetizers, not the main course!

Un plat is a dish that is being served. *Le plat principal* is the main course. In a restaurant, *les plats principaux* are the choice of main courses.

Finally, at a restaurant, *le plat du jour* is the specialty of the day. It is often not on the printed menu, but on a chalkboard instead. If it's a restaurant that has a limited menu that's new every day, *le plat du jour* is what they are serving today.

c'est comme ça

This little expression means <u>That's the way it is</u>. As with its English counterpart, it conveys a sense of inevitability.

La vie, c'est comme ça,.

That's the way life is. / Life is like that.

Quand le temps est mauvais j'ai mal par-
tout, mais c'est comme ça.

When the weather is bad I ache all over,
but that's the way it is.

défense de
défendu de
interdit
gênant

Défense de, défendu and ***interdit*** are expressions
that you need to know and recognize when you see
them on signs because these are the words that
mean that something is <u>prohibited or forbidden</u>.

Gênant means <u>in the way</u> or <u>blocking the road</u>, and
if you see that on the sign it means forbidden as
well. (We discussed the verb *gêner* earlier).

Here are some examples:

Défense de se garer ici ! / Stationnement
défendu ! / Parking interdit ! / Il est défen-
du de stationner ici !

Parking here is forbidden / No parking!

Stationnement gênant !

"If you park here you are in the way and
blocking the road, and we are going to
tow you away if we see you".

Défense de fumer.

No smoking.

Il est défendu de parler au chauffeur.

Don't talk to the driver / It's forbidden to talk to the driver.

Affichage interdit.

No posting of signs.

Entrée formellement / strictement interdite (au public).

Entrance strictly prohibited (to the public). (As a cultural note, a francophone friend told me that adding *formellement* or *strictement* will make a French person take it more seriously.)

de l'eau du robinet
une carafe (d'eau)

Restaurants in France don't automatically put water on the table for you the way restaurants do in the States. You will likely be asked *De l'eau plate ou de l'eau gazeuse ?* (Water without bubbles or with bubbles?), when your order is taken.

It sounds very innocent, as if *"l'eau plate"* is ordinary drinking water, but watch out! If you accept the invitation for *l'eau plate,* you'll get a bottle of of brand-name bottled water and you will be billed up to four or five euros for each bottle you drink.

Now, some people do prefer to drink bottled water. And restaurants prefer to serve you a high-profit item which costs them 20-30 cents and they can sell you for fifteen or twenty times that. However, if you are like me and are content with ordinary drinking water (this is France, after all, with one of the best health and sanitation systems in the world), you need to specify it.

The trick is to ask for *une carafe d'eau,* or just *une carafe*, or if you want to be absolutely clear, *de l'eau du robinet.*

> *De l'eau plate ou de l'eau gazeuse ? --- Une carafe, s'il vous plaît / De l'eau du robinet, s'il vous plaît.*

> Bottled water without bubbles or with? --- A carafe of ordinary drinking water, if you please.

The fanciest restaurant will serve you a carafe of water if you ask for it. (They are obliged to by French law, and they are used to it). If you see the waiter coming with bottled water in spite of your request, just say *Non, j'ai demandé de l'eau du robinet.*

This section has saved you at least the cost of this entire book.

des ennuis

In English, ennui is a rather refined and literary word for boredom. In French, on the other hand, while *en-*

nui can also mean boredom when used in a literary sense, you are unlikely to encounter this meaning. What you will hear is the frequent use of **des ennuis** for <u>worries</u> or for <u>problems</u>.

Elle a beaucoup d'ennuis.

She has a lot of worries / problems.

Il a des ennuis d'argent.

He has money problems / worries.

Il a des ennuis de santé.

He has problems with his health / worries with his health.

Ne fais pas ça ! / Il faut pas faire ça ! Tu vas avoir des ennuis.

Don't do that. You are going to have problems (because of it).

Tu t'attires des ennuis / Il s'attire des ennuis.

You are bringing problems on yourself / He's bringing problems on himself.

Note that *ennuis* can be either the problems or the worries caused by the problems, but they usually mean both together. In other words, *des ennuis* usually refer to both the problems and the worries they cause, together.

Des ennuis is a common expression that you will hear frequently and use yourself.

foutu

I told you earlier that we had reached the end of our curse words, but I was wrong. We can't quit without including **foutu**. *Foutu*, which is considered vulgar, has a number of senses, but the most common meanings, and the ones that you are most likely to hear, are first <u>damn,</u> and secondly <u>ruined or finished</u>.

As <u>damn</u>, *foutu* is used fairly similarly to *putain de* which we discussed above. They are both considered vulgar by the way. Note that in this usage the *foutu* is always <u>before</u> the noun.

> **Ce foutu chat a fait beaucoup de dégâts /
> Ce putain de chat... / Ce sale chat...**
>
>> That damn cat made a lot of mess / did a lot of damage.
>
> **Ce foutu téléphone ! Il n'arrête pas de sonner !**
>
>> This damn telephone! It doesn't quit ringing!
>
> **J'en ai assez de cette foutue pluie !**
>
>> I've had enough of this damn rain!
>
> **Je peux pas faire démarrer cette foutue bagnole !**

I can't get this damn car started

Here are some uses of *foutu* as <u>ruined, finished or broken down</u>. Here the foutu is <u>after</u> the noun.

Je suis foutu !

I've had it / I'm up a creek / I'm done for!

Ma bagnole est foutue.

My car has had it / is done for.

La mayonnaise est foutue.

The mayonnaise is spoiled / The mayonnaise didn't come out the way it was supposed to.

Ça a bien marché hier, mais maintenant c'est foutu.

It worked great yesterday, but now it's broken / but now it doesn't work.

You may wonder why a word which you translate by damn or busted should be considered so vulgar. Well it's as if you said "that fucked up car", or "now it's all fucked up". What you mean to say is just that it's busted or annoying, but you've employed a vulgar word to say so.

It's exactly the same if you say *cette foutue voiture* because the old meaning of the verb **foutre** was to screw or fuck, (although that meaning is currently considered dated).

In current slang, the verb *foutre* means <u>to do</u>, and thus is a very slangy way to say *faire:*

> ### Est-ce qu'il n'a rien d'autre à foutre ?
>
> Doesn't he have anything else to do?
>
> ### Qu'est-ce qu'elle fout? Ça fait une heure qu'on l'attend.
>
> What is she doing? That makes an hour that we are waiting for her.
>
> ### Ne me tracasse pas avec ça, on a autre chose à foutre.
>
> Don't bug me with that. We've got other things to do.

Side Note: You may be wondering how *foutre*, which used to mean to fuck, ever came to mean to do. It's interesting to note that fuck has followed the same course in English:

> What's he fucking around with? = What's he doing?
>
> We've got better things to fuck around with! = We've got better things to do!

Thus *Est-ce qu'il n'a rien d'autre à foutre ?* which we translated above as "Doesn't he have anything else to do?" could be translated slangily as "Doesn't he have anything else to fuck around with?", as *foutre* is clearly a very slangy word.

fichu

Fichu is a milder word which can be used in most of the same ways as *foutu*. It is not considered vulgar but is certainly *familier*. Here are some examples of its use:

> **Ce fichu chat a fait beaucoup de dégâts.**
>
> **Je peux pas faire démarrer cette fichue bagnole !**
>
> **Je suis fichu !**
>
> **Ça a bien marché hier, mais maintenant c'est fichu.**

Side Note: Earlier on, we discussed *Je m'en fiche* and *Je m'en fous* which both mean "I don't give a damn about it". The verb infinitives are *ficher* and *foutre*. The words *fichu* and *foutu,* which we have just discussed here, are the past participles of these verbs.

sale

Another common French word which has some similarities to *fichu* and *foutre*, and one which is usually not considered vulgar, is **sale**. *Sale* literally means <u>dirty</u> (not in the sense of pornography, but in the sense of dirt), but when used as an epithet, and <u>before</u> the noun, it means <u>damn, darned, nasty, disagreeable, repugnant, or worse</u>. For example:

Ce sale chat a fait beaucoup de dégâts.

That darn cat has made a big mess.

C'est une sale affaire.

It's a nasty business. (Corrupt, dangerous, whatever).

C'est un sale type.

The meaning of this can range from "He's a nasty, disagreeable guy" to "He's a real bastard!" *(un salaud !* which also comes from *sale). * You can usually tell just how nasty the speaker wished to portray the *sale type* by context, emphasis, and tone of voice.

Elle a malheureusement une sale maladie.

Unfortunately she has a nasty / serious / grave illness with poor prognosis.

Je peux pas faire démarrer cette sale bagnole !

Note that this means "I can't get this damn car started" and doesn't mean "I can't start this broken car". *Sale* **never** means busted or done for, as *fichu* or *foutu* might.

Time words: We are now going to discuss a small group of words having to do with order in time. These are the French equivalents of the English words **again, since, already, for (an amount of time), yet, how long, etc**. These, again, are little words that you'll use frequently.

encore

We'll start with the adverb *encore*, which has a number of related meanings. This is a very, very common word that you really will use every day – multiple times.

First, *encore* as <u>still</u> in the sense of <u>a continuing state or action</u>.

> ***Il est encore étudiant / enfant / célibataire.***
>
> He is still a student / a child / unmarried.
>
> ***Il travaille encore à l'usine / comme médecin.***
>
> He still works at the factory / He still works as a doctor.
>
> ***Est-ce qu'il reste encore à Paris ?***
>
> Is he still in Paris?
>
> ***Est-ce qu'elle est encore en train de cuisiner ?***
>
> Is she still doing her cooking?

In negative sentences *encore* can mean <u>yet</u>.

> ***Il n'est pas encore arrivé.***

He hasn't arrived yet.

Pas encore.

Not yet.

Je n'ai pas encore fini.

I haven't finished yet.

Encore can also mean <u>again</u>.

J'irai encore la semaine prochaine.

I'll go again next week.

Je l'ai encore vu la semaine dernière.

I saw him again last week.

Et encore une fois cette semaine.

And again one time this week / And one time more this week.

And this multifaceted word, *encore,* can also mean <u>more</u>.

Encore du vin, s'il vous plaît.

More wine, please.

En voulez-vous encore ?

Would you like more of it?

Quoi encore ?

What more? / What now? (said with exasperation)

Finally, *encore* can be used to intensify. You could translate it as <u>still</u> or <u>even</u>, in these cases.

Elle est encore plus belle que sa soeur.

She is <u>even</u> more beautiful than her sister / She is <u>still</u> more beautiful…

C'est encore mieux.

That's <u>even</u> better.

Rather than trying to memorize all the meanings for *encore*, it will probably be better to read over the example sentences two or three times to get a feeling for the sense of *encore* in different contexts. In fact, you can often tell the meaning from the context.

depuis

The preposition *depuis* is another very common time word. It usually means <u>since</u>. It is proper French and it's used all the time.

First of all, *depuis* can mean <u>since</u> in the sense of <u>since a point in time</u>.

Je vis à New York depuis 1990.

I have lived in New York since 1990.

Elle est malade depuis juin.

She has been sick since June.

Je ne suis pas sorti depuis la semaine dernière.

I haven't gone out since last week.

Depuis quand ?

Since when?

Depuis quand est-ce que tu la connais ?

How long have you known her? (Since when...?)

In English we say I have lived in New York <u>since</u> 1990, but I have lived in New York <u>for</u> fifteen years. The difference is that the first refers to a point of departure in time and we say <u>since then</u>, and the second refers to a passage of a certain amount of time and we say <u>for that time</u>. **In French,** *depuis* is used for both, and in both cases it means that the condition still exists:

Je vis à New York depuis 1990.

I have lived in New York <u>since</u> 1990.

Je vis à New York depuis quinze ans.

I have lived in New York <u>for</u> fifteen years.

Note that <u>if the situation no longer exists</u> (if you no longer live in New York), you use *pendant* as in:

J'ai vécu à New York pendant quinze ans.

I lived in New York for fifteen years.

or <u>if you are naming the dates</u> you can use one of these structures:

J'ai vécu à New York de 1990 à 2005.

Je vivais à New York dans les années avant 2000.

Here are some more examples of *depuis* referring to <u>a passage of time</u>. It's usually translated as <u>for</u>.

Je suis malade depuis huit jours.

I have been sick <u>for</u> eight days.

Je l'aime depuis toujours.

I've loved her (or him) <u>for</u>ever / I've always loved her.

Depuis combien de temps es-tu à la fac ?

How long have you been at the university. (For how much time…)

Depuis can also refer to <u>places and numbers</u>.

Il y avait des bouchons sur l'autoroute depuis Montpelier.

There were traffic jams on the autoroute all the way from Montpelier / We were in bumper-to-bumper traffic ever since Montpelier.

Depuis la cuisine, maman peut entendre tout dans la maison.

From the kitchen mommy can hear everything in the house.

Ils ont des pantalons depuis 50 euros jusqu'à 150 euros. (It would probably be easier and simpler to say *Ils ont des pantalons de 50 à 150 euros*, but the use of depuis is also correct.)

They have pants from 50 euros to 150 euros.

You may occasionally hear *depuis* as an adverb, but you may not notice that it's any different unless you are a grammarian. (It's also translated with <u>since</u>).

Je l'ai vu en juin, mais je ne l'ai pas vu depuis.

I saw him in June, but I haven't seen him since.

déjà

Next in our "time" words we have ***déjà***, which means <u>already</u>. At the risk of repeating myself, all these time words are frequently encountered, and you'll find occasion to use them yourself frequently too,

J'ai déjà trop à faire.

I already have too much to do.

Il est déjà six heures.

It's already six o'clock

Il est déjà temps de partir.

It's already time to leave.

Déjà can also be used to intensify:

Cinq cents euros, c'est déjà pas mal.

Five hundred euros, that's not bad already.

S'il a avoué ça, c'est déjà quelque chose.

If he's admitted that much, that's already something / that's something at least.

And don't forget the additional "time" words and expressions that we have already discussed earlier in this book such as: *enfin* (finally), *ensuite* and *par la suite* (next), *toujours*, (always), *entre-temps* (meanwhile), *après coup* (afterwards), *tout à l'heure* (in a little while or a little while ago), and others.

Pardon !
Pardonnez-moi !
Excusez-moi !
Excuse-moi !
Mille excuses !
Mes excuses !
Désolé !
Je suis désolé.
Je suis navré de...

These are very key expressions. They are different ways to say that you are sorry!

Excusez-moi and *excuse-moi* are straightforward:

Excusez-moi !

Excuse me! (In threading through people at the supermarket, or to excuse yourself after having bumped someone inadvertently)

Excuse-moi !

(Used with someone with whom you are on a *tu* basis).

Excusez-moi d'être en retard.

Excuse me for being late.

Excusez-nous d'être en retard.

Excuse us for being late.

Mille excuses ! is a bit different. It uses the noun *excuses* instead of the verb *excuser* and literally means "A thousand excuses". You can use it in threading your way through a crowd, or to make your excuses for being late.

Mille excuses d'être en retard.

Mes excuses ! is shortened from the much more formal *Je vous présente mes excuses.* It is never used to alert people at the supermarket or on the sidewalk but is used to say you are sorry. It's less casual than *Excusez-moi.*

Mes excuses d'être en retard.

My daughter says that among close friends and family it can even be shortened further to just *Excuses !*

Pardon and ***pardonnez-moi*** are very similar. *Pardon !*, too, is often used to warn someone in a crowd, to attract someones attention, etc.

I was puzzled when I first came across *Pardon !* as it didn't fit any tense of the verb *pardonner*. I then figured out that it is the noun *pardon* and that *Pardon !* was long ago abbreviated from *Je vous demande pardon !* (I beg your pardon!). It's probably used even more frequently than *Excusez-moi !* You'll walk through crowds saying *Pardon... Pardon... Pardon... Pardon...*

You can also use *Pardon ?* as a question if you didn't quite hear what someone said:

Il a...et après ça... (half-heard) --- Pardon ?

He has...and after that...(half-heard) --- Excuse me! What did you say?

However, the noun *pardon* and *pardonnez-moi* can also be used to say that you are sorry about something you've done, which is a different meaning if you think about. For example:

Je vous demande pardon. J'ai fait quelque chose de vraiment stupide / J'ai vraiment fait une bêtise.

Please forgive me. I did something really stupid.

Pourrais-tu me pardonner ? Ce que j'ai dit est une grosse bêtise.

Can you forgive me? What I said was really stupid.

Je suis désolé also can be translated with sorry but it has a different sense and usage.

The verb *désoler* means to distress or grieve if applied to a person, and *désolé* means desolate or devastated if applied to a landscape.

Thus, by exaggeration, *Je suis désolé* means I'm sorry in the sense of I'm very distressed, I'm grieved, or I'm desolate (to hear about..., because of...).

If you think of *Excusez-moi* as meaning sorry in the sense of Excuse me, and *Pardonnez-moi* as meaning sorry in the sense of Pardon me, you can see that *Je suis désolé* really means something different.

> **Ma fille a beaucoup d'ennuis avec son travail. --- Oh ! Je suis désolé ! Est-ce que je peux faire quelque chose ?**
>
> My daughter has a lot of problems with her work. --- Oh! I'm really sorry / grieved / distressed (to hear it). Is there anything that I can do?

> **Je suis désolé d'être autant en retard.**
>
> I'm very sorry / distressed to be so very late.

Je suis désolé is sometimes abbreviated as just **Désolé**, but in this case it's more casual.

> **Désolé d'être en retard.** (When you are just ten minutes late, for example, and you are talking to a friend).

Désolé or *Je suis désolé* can also be used as a form of <u>contradiction</u>:

> **Désolé, mais ce n'est pas une bonne idée !**
>
> Sorry to tell you this, / Sorry to disagree, but it's not a good idea! (**Pardon, mais...** can be used in the same way).

Je suis navré is another expression that says that you are upset or distressed. While it's used in spoken French, it's more formal than *Je suis désolé* and less frequently encountered. You are more likely to hear *Je suis navré* in more formal situations.

> **Je suis navré d'apprendre que votre fille soit malade.**
>
>> I am distressed / very sorry to learn that your daughter is ill.
>
> **Nous sommes navrés d'avoir fait attendre tout le monde / de vous avoir fait attendre.**
>
>> We are distressed / sorry to have kept everyone waiting / to have made you wait..

To summarize: These expressions are sometimes interchangeable, but at other times, and in other situations, not interchangeable at all. For example, in walking through a crowd you can alert people that you are there by saying *Excusez-moi* or *Pardon* or even *Mille excuses*. However, saying *Je suis désolé* or *Je suis navré* just wouldn't fit at all. That's not what they are for.

On the other hand if you inadvertently bump someone you can say any one of these four:

> **Excusez-moi ! Je vous ai pas vu / Pardon ! Je vous ai pas vu / Désolé ! Je vous ai pas vu / Mille excuses ! Je....**
>
>> Sorry, I didn't see you.

However, *Je suis navré* might be too serious and too formal for this situation, except perhaps if you had really bumped someone hard, and maybe knocked them down, and you wanted to emphasize that you were sincerely apologizing.

If you need to make a more formal <u>apology</u>, you can try one of the following:

> **Je vous présente mes excuses.**
>
> **Je vous demande pardon.**
>
> **Je suis très navré** *(d'avoir dit cela, de vous avoir bousculé, etc).*

Finally, if someone tells you that their daughter is ill, you could say you are <u>sorry to hear it</u> with **Je suis désolé** or **Je suis navré** but not of course with *Excusez-moi* or *Pardon*.

je suis égaré
je suis perdu

These expressions are really important because they are <u>how you say you are lost</u>. You should memorize them so well that you can say them when you need them without having to think about it.

> **Pardon. Je suis égaré. Je cherche L'Hôtel de la Gare.**
>
> **Pardon. Je suis perdu. Je cherche L'Hôtel de la Gare.**

Excuse me. I'm lost. I'm looking for L'Hôtel de la Gare.

And to really get someone's attention, the magic sentence is:

Excusez-moi de vous déranger mais je suis perdu. Je cherche...

Sorry to bother you but I'm lost. I'm looking for...

un feu rouge

Un feu rouge isn't a red fire. It's a red light, a red traffic light. In fact, almost all lights having to do with cars and roads are called *feux* instead of *lumières*. For example, *les feux arrières* are the tail lights, and *feux de brouillard* are fog lights. *(Un feu vert* is of course a green light. And in French, instead of referring to a yellow traffic light, you say *un feu orange).*

Tournez à gauche au premier feu rouge.

Turn left at the first red light.

comme vous voulez
comme tu veux

The expression *comme vous voulez* means as you wish. It's a common expression and a way of assenting.

Comme vous voulez sometimes can imply that you

are tired of discussing the issue or tired of arguing about it.

> **Mais c'est mieux de le faire comme je vous l'ai expliqué ! --- Comme vous voulez.**
>
>> But it's better to do it the way I explained to you! --- As you wish. (With a sense of resignation).

However *comme vous voulez* can also simply mean that you are letting the other person decide. It depends on context and tone of voice.

> **Est-ce que vous préférez un rouge ou un rosé ? --- Comme vous voulez.**
>
>> Would you prefer a red wine or a rosé? --- As you wish / You choose! (With a sense of courtesy, rather than resignation).

If you are on a *tu* basis, you say *comme tu veux*.

> **Mais c'est mieux de le faire comme je te l'ai expliqué ! --- Comme tu veux.**

You will sometimes hear <u>C'est</u> *comme vous voulez* or <u>C'est</u> *comme tu veux*. (*Comme vous voulez* is actually probably an abbreviation of *C'est comme vous voulez*).

> **Est-ce que vous préférez un rouge ou un rosé ? --- C'est comme vous voulez.**

jouer aux cartes

This section provides a bit of vocabulary for those who play cards. The way you say to play cards is **jouer aux cartes**. A deck of cards, if you want to buy one, is **un jeu de cartes.**

The suits are called **couleurs**, and they are **piques** (spades), **coeurs** (hearts), **carreaux** (diamonds), and **trèfles** (clubs). (The actual meaning of *une pique* is a pike, the weapon; the meaning of *un coeur* is a heart, of course; the meaning of *un carreau* is a floor tile, window pane or checked fabric; the meaning of *un trèfle* is a three-leaf clover. The club symbol on playing cards actually resembles a three-leaf clover a lot more than it resembles a club).

A king is **un roi** and the symbol on the corner of the card is *R*, (not K as it is in an English language deck). A queen is **une dame**, symbol *D*. A jack is **un valet**, symbol *V*. An ace is **un as**, and the symbol is *1* (not *A).*

mot de passe

In this world of computers and digital accessories, this is an expression you should know. It means password.

Tapez votre mot de passe.

Enter your password.

All French charge cards have computer chips in

them and you enter your code instead of signing your name as in the US at present. You'll be asked to enter your code:

Tapez votre code.

les grandes surfaces
un hypermarché

Les grandes surfaces refers to <u>big stores</u>, with large selling areas, like supermarkets, department stores, big hardware stores, and the equivalents of Wal-Mart™ and Target™.

Some *grandes surfaces* are *supermarchés* and *hypermarchés*. **Un supermarché** is a supermarket. **Un hypermarché** is like a superstore. It can be a big supermarket, or a hardware and home furnishings store, or it can be a specialized store like a *un hypermarché de chaussures* (which sells just shoes), or whatever. *À la grande surface* is an expression you'll hear a lot and will use yourself fairly often.

Je n'ai pas trouvé des mangues chez l'épicier. Je vais essayer en grande surface / au supermarché.

I couldn't find mangos at the little grocery store. I'm going to try at the *grande surface* (supermarket).

Je l'ai acheté à la grande surface.

I bought it at *la grande surface* (There is

no single equivalent word in English. It means you bought it at a big Wal-Mart™ type store or at a large supermarket.)

payer en liquide
payer en espèces

En liquide or *en espèces* mean in cash, and **payer en liquide** or **payer en espèces** mean to pay in cash.

These expressions are important to know as you will sometimes be asked to pay in cash by someone who doesn't want to be paid by check, for instance. This may be because he is working without declaring the income for taxes. At other times you may be able to negotiate a better price on something you buy if you offer to pay *en liquide.*

> **Est-ce que vous pouvez payer en liquide / en espèces.**

> Can you pay in cash.

> **Je peux payer en liquide / en espèces.**

> I can pay in cash.

Subjectively, I think that there is a subtle difference in the use of the two expressions. The difference is that *espèces* is a neutral word that simply means in cash, in bills, in money (as opposed to paying by check or charge card). On the other hand, *en liquide* has a possible implication that one is not going to declare the money on taxes. It has a vague hint of illicit about it. For example:

> **Notre lecteur est en panne. Il faut payer par chèque ou en espèces.**

> Our credit card reader isn't working. You have to pay by check or cash. (You would not use *en liquide* here).

> **Il travaille au noir. Il faut le payer en liquide.**

> He doesn't declare his income. You have to pay him in cash. (Here you would probably use *en liquide* but you could also conceivably use *en espèces* as it's neutral and just means in cash).

un jour de fête
les vacances
le congé

These are holiday words. **Un jour de fête** is a (national) holiday, like *le quatorze juillet* (which we call Bastille Day). There are also a myriad of religious *jours de fête* in France when most everything closes down.

> **Les grandes surfaces vont être fermées demain. C'est un jour de fête.**

> The big stores will be closed tomorrow. It's a holiday. (They close on *jours de fête*, and some are closed on Sun-

days as well. Neighborhood stores and stores in smaller towns and villages often close one day a week, often Monday or Wednesday, and also usually close every day between noon and two for lunch).

On the other hand, *les vacances* usually refer to scheduled vacation time. Note that it is a plural word). For example:

les vacances d'été

summer vacation or holiday

Il faut pas conduire ce samedi. C'est le début des vacances scolaires.

We shouldn't drive this Saturday. It's the beginning of the school holidays (The roads will be jammed).

Il vient de partir en vacances.

He just left on vacation.

Il va passer ses vacances au bord de la mer.

He is going to spend his vacation on the coast.

Tu as l'air fatigué. Prends des vacances.

You look tired. Take some vacation.

Le congé on the other hand, while it can mean vacation, usually means something more like time off.

Elle est en congé de formation / en congé de maternité.

> She's off work to go to a training session / She's on maternity leave.

Il prend une semaine de congé.

> He's taking a week of leave / of vacation.

However, ***donner son congé*** means <u>to give notice</u> that one is quitting, or it can mean to give an employee notice. The difference in meaning is always evident from the context. For example:

Elle a donné / a remis son congé au patron.

> She gave the boss her notice (that she was quitting).

Son patron lui a donné son congé.

> Her boss gave her notice that he was letting her go.

Finally, the verb ***congédier*** means to <u>dismiss</u> someone from your presence, to send them away, or to fire an employee.

Elle a été congédiée / licenciée.

> She was fired.

doué

The adjective **doué** means <u>gifted or talented</u>. It's not a slang expression but is good French.

Elle est douée en maths.

She's gifted in math.

C'est un étudiant doué pour les sciences.

He's a student who is specially talented in science.

Elle est douée d'une forte intelligence.

She is gifted with an impressive intelligence.

However, in common speech, *doué* is often used <u>ironically</u>. This is, in fact, the way you are likely to hear it used most commonly.

For example: You drop a project on the floor that you and your friend have been working hard on. It's now scattered and the two of you have to pick it up off the floor. He or she might say something like:

Oh ! T'es vraiment doué, toi !

Oh! You are really talented ! (Note that I abbreviated *Tu es* as *T'es* here. This is definitely not proper French, but in the heat of the moment, with the project on the floor, it's probably how an annoyed

French person would say it. Especially a young person or student.)

fort

Another way to say that someone is <u>especially talented</u> is to use the adjective **fort**. For example:

> **Il est fort en maths / Elle est forte en anglais.**
>
> > He's very strong (talented) in math. / She is strong (talented) in English.
>
> **Il est fort aux échecs.**
>
> > He's talented at chess. (It's *fort <u>à</u>* if you are referring to a game).
>
> **C'est un brave homme, mais il n'est pas bien fort.**
>
> > He's a nice guy but he's not very bright (or talented).

messieurs dames

When entering a room (or even a bakery or other shop) where there are mixed men and women, or even when encountering another group of hikers on a walking trail, a French person will usually say:

> **Bonjour, messieurs dames.**

This translates pretty close to "Good day, ladies and gentlemen".

Bonjour, messieurs dames is short for *Bonjour, messieurs et mesdames* (which no one actually ever says any more). All the letters usually aren't even pronounced and it comes out as something like:

Bonjour, m'sieu dames.

Of course, if you entered a room in which there were just women you'd say:

Bonjour, mesdames.

and if there were just men:

Bonjour, messieurs.

Note that in English on entering a room we'd probably just say "Hello, everybody", on entering a shop with other shoppers in it that we didn't know we probably wouldn't say anything, and in passing someone on a hiking trail we probably wouldn't say more than "Hi", or nod and say "Nice day".

Side Note: For a little word on *messieurs* and *mesdames*: *monsieur* is a pushing together of *mon* and *sieur* which means something like "my sir", and *madame* is a combination of *ma* and *dame* which is "my lady". Thus, when you are addressing several people, the plural of *madame* is usually not *madames* but *mesdames (mes dames)*, and the plural of *monsieur* is *messieurs*.

And by the way:

Monsieur is abbreviated *M*.

Messieurs is abbreviated *MM*.

Madame is abbreviated *Mme*

Mademoiselle is abbreviated *Mlle*. (It is never pronounced "mamzel" as it often is in English, but is usually "madmwazel" at least).

Also note that while a generic *monsieur* or *madame* is not capitalized, if you refer to a specific person, such as *Monsieur Blanchet,* it is capitalized.

I hope that you really enjoyed this book. I also hope that it wasn't only useful, but that it was interesting and entertaining as well. That was half the point of it, after all.

List of References

I used the following reference books to supplement my knowledge from everyday reading and conversation in the preparation of this book.

Harper Collins French Concise Dictionary, Second Edition, Harper Collins, 2000

Harrap's Shorter Dictionnaire, Anglais-Français Français-Anglais, 7th Edition, Chambers Harrap, 2004

Webster's New World Dictionary, Second College Edition, Simon and Schuster, 1982

Le Petit Robert, Dictionnaire Alphabétique et Analogique de la Langue Française, Dictionnaires Le Robert, 1993

Le Petit Larousse, Grand Format, Larousse, 2001

Dictionary 1.0.1, Apple Computer 2005

Alphabetical Listing

In alphabetizing, when *un* is just part of the noun, like *un truc*, I alphabetize it under the noun (here, for example, under T for *truc*). However, when the *un* is an integral part of the expression, such as *un point c'est tout,* or *un drôle de*, or even *une carafe !* (when asking for water)*,* I alphabetize it under U for *un*. My reasoning was that if you are looking for *truc*, you'd certainly look under T, but if you were looking for the expression *un point c'est tout*, you'd likely look under U.

Please note also that in this index I used **all lower case first letters** even when the first letter would ordinarliy be capitalized. For example *Pardon !* is listed as *pardon !* This is done simply to be easier on the eye and to make it easier for you to spot what you are looking for.

LaVergne, TN USA
10 October 2010
200269LV00004B/79/P